STARTING MONDAY

by Anne Commire

SAMUEL FRENCH, INC.
45 WEST 25TH STREET   NEW YORK 10010
7623 SUNSET BOULEVARD HOLLYWOOD 90046
LONDON   TORONTO

Copyright © 1989, 1991 by Anne Commire

ALL RIGHTS RESERVED

CAUTION: Professionals and amateurs are hereby warned that STARTING MONDAY is subject to a royalty. It is fully protected under the copyright laws of the United States of America, the British Commonwealth, including Canada, and all other countries of the Copyright Union. All rights, including professional, amateur, motion pictures, recitation, lecturing, public reading, radio broadcasting, television, and the rights of translation into foreign languages are strictly reserved. In its present form the play is dedicated to the reading public only.

The amateur live stage performance rights to STARTING MONDAY are controlled exclusively by Samuel French, Inc., and royalty arrangements and licenses must be secured well in advance of presentation. PLEASE NOTE that amateur royalty fees are set upon application in accordance with your producing circumstances. When applying for a royalty quotation and license please give us the number of performances intended, dates of production, your seating capacity and admission fee. Royalties are payable one week before the opening performance of the play to Samuel French, Inc., at 45 W. 25th Street, New York, NY 10010; or at 7623 Sunset Blvd., Hollywood, CA 90046, or to Samuel French (Canada), Ltd., 80 Richmond Street East, Toronto, Ontario, Canada M5C 1P1.

Royalty of the required amount must be paid whether the play is presented for charity or gain and whether or not admission is charged.

Stock royalty quoted on application to Samuel French, Inc.

For all other rights than those stipulated above, apply to Joyce Ketay, 334 West 89th Street, New York, NY 10024.

Particular emphasis is laid on the question of amateur or professional readings, permission and terms for which must be secured in writing from Samuel French, Inc.

Copying from this book in whole or in part is strictly forbidden by law, and the right of performance is not transferable.

Whenever the play is produced the following notice must appear on all programs, printing and advertising for the play: "Produced by special arrangement with Samuel French, Inc."

Due authorship credit must be given on all programs, printing and advertising for the play.

ISBN 0 573 69232 7   Printed in U.S.A.

*For Merrily, whose every troubled breath
gave this play life.*

For Sara Botsford, who knew the melody.

No one shall commit or authorize any act or omission by which the copyright of, or the right to copyright, this play may be impaired.

No one shall make any changes in this play for the purpose of production.

Publication of this play does not imply availability for performance. Both amateurs and professionals considering a production are *strongly* advised in their own interests to apply to Samuel French, Inc., for written permission before starting rehearsals, advertising, or booking a theatre.

No part of this book may be reproduced, stored in a retrieval system, or transmitted in any form, by any means, now known or yet to be invented, including mechanical, electronic, photocopying, recording, videotaping, or otherwise, without the prior written permission of the publisher.

IMPORTANT BILLING AND CREDIT REQUIREMENTS

All producers of STARTING MONDAY *must* give credit to the Author of the Play in all programs distributed in connection with performances of the Play and in all instances in which the title of the Play appears for purposes of advertising, publicizing or otherwise exploiting the Play and/or a production. The name of the Author *must* also appear on a separate line, on which no other name appears, immediately following the title, and *must* appear in size of type equal to the largest letter used for the title of the play. The following acknowledgment must appear on the first page of credit in all programs distributed in connection with performances of the play:

> *Starting Monday* was given a staged reading at the 1983 National Playwrights Conference at the O'Neill Theatre Center.
>
> First produced in "Winterfest" at the Yale Repertory Theatre.
>
> New York City premiere presented by the WPA Theatre in March, 1990, Kyle Renick Producer.

Starting Monday was first presented in Waterford, Conn. at the 1988 Eugene O'Neill National Playwright's Conference (with Linda Hunt, Deborah Hedwall, Ellen Parker, Kaiulani Lee, Helen Stenborg, Kirk Jackson, Patrick Kerr, Polly Draper. Amy Saltz directing.) It was subsequently produced in Winterfest at the Yale Repertory Theatre with the following cast:

LYNNE	Sara Botsford
ELLIS	Leslie Lyles
GERMAN, and OTHERS	C. Phillips Kaufman
DR. BENBERG, and OTHERS	Charles Bartlett
HELEN	Sylvia Short
NURSE EATON	Mary Louise Wilson
TRISH	Rosalyn Coleman
FARMER'S WIFE, and OTHERS	Babo Harrison
ORDERLIES	Jim MacLaren
	Michael W. McCarty

Director:	Peter Mark Shifter
Dramaturg:	Ernie Schier
Set Designer:	Sarah Lambert
Costume Designer:	Nephelie Andonyadis
Lighting Designer:	David Birn
Stage Manager:	Robin Rumpf
Production Dramaturg:	Steven S. Oxman
Artistic Director:	Lloyd Richards

Starting Monday was first produced in New York City in March 1990 at the WPA Theatre. The cast (in order of appearance) was:

LYNNE	Pamela Wiggins
ELLIS	Ellen Greene
GERMAN and OTHERS	Ilo Orleans
DR. BENBERG and OTHERS	David Manis
HELEN	Patricia O'Connell
NURSE EATON	Paddy Croft
PATIENT IN WHEELCHAIR	Ilo Orleans
TRISH	Pamela Tucker-White
FARMER'S WIFE and OTHERS	Susan Brenner

Director:	Zina Jasper
Setting by	Edward T. Gianfrancesco
Lighting by	Craig Evans
Costumes by	Mimi Maxmen
Sound by	Aural Fixation
Stage Manager:	Jana Llynn
Producer:	Kyle Renick

CHARACTERS

Lynne

Ellis

Man, One German, Doctor in Surgery Garb, Dr. Benberg, LA Cop, Technician

Jim, Another German, Male Nurse, Patient in Wheelchair, Farmer, Skycap

Helen

Nurse Eaton

Trish

Nurse, Mrs. Koenig, Farmer's Wife, Blood Nurse

TIME

11:00 a.m.

PLACE

New York City

Production Notes

The set should consist of three PLAYING AREAS with levels or modules for sitting, lounging, and prop containment. The main focal area contains a bed with headboard an elective variable to suggest different locales. [In some productions a hospital bed has been used, disguised with mock headboards or cloth coverlets, until hospital scenes in Act II. The bed might also be on a pivot to allow for quick position changes. It would also be helpful if US side of bed had compartments for cast off props.] The bed will be underdressed with spreads and blankets. Thus, a change of scene can be accomplished with the removal of the top spread. Also, actresses may enter wrapped in the described bedding: messy sheets, quilts, etc. The bed is accompanied by a nondescript bed table (US of it) and a chair. Headphones (no cords) have a permanent position on the bedpost. PLAYING AREA 2 contains a bench with US shelving to contain props. PLAYING AREA 3 is neutral.

Props should be representational, used only for the sake of definition or the comfort of actors. They should never be complete, i.e. use preset drawings on sketch pads, mime crayons; use journal, mime pencil; use coffee mugs, mime liquid; use grocery bag, mime contents; use clipboards, mime paper; headphones, no cords. Wherever romanized within italics, props should not be used at all. Lynne is the beast of burden: arranging scenery, carrying props on and off. Ellis wafts through Lynne's memory. If the amount of props become ludicrous, if Lynne looks like an overloaded pack horse, she should play this with the audience.

Similarly, costumes should be changed only to make a point, not to suggest change of day. As much as the script and the director are limited to the use of props to keep the pace, ditto the costume designer. Since Lynne is narrating the story, she should have a base attire, changed only by the addition or subtraction of a blazer or sweater, etc.

It will be tempting to visit the local hospital for accuracy. Remember three things: (1) This play takes place in the early '80s. (2) Medical procedures vary with locale. (3) The medical ephemera need not be complete, (i.e. representational ointment, no goop). The changing of the dressing scene is by necessity abridged.

Because of complexities of the play, stage directions should be followed; or, at least read. In one production blackouts were inserted between each scene, adding 35 minutes to the playing time. There should be very few blackouts: the end of Act I and Act II; the end of scene one and two. Those first two "hangover" scenes should be treated as a prologue—with the second scene creating the illusion that it's about Lynne a year later, until Ellis pops up.

ACT I

AT RISE: SOUND: Strains of "Auld Lang Syne."
Slatted LIGHT streams from the fourth-wall window illuminating the bed. A blanket covers the vitals of an over-35-year-old lump; a pillow covers its head. There is a phone on the bed table; a man's shoe, sock, and shirt are on the floor. The PHONE rings, the lump extends an arm from the swaddling clothes in one-quarter time; picks up the phone slowly. As MUSIC fades, ANNOUNCER blends in with: "1978! HAPPY NEW YEAR, EVERYBODY!"

LYNNE. (*Groans something resembling:*) Hello ... (*Eyes like mail slots.*) What time is it? What year? Don't tell me, I don't want to know; I feel awful ... A party at Doubleday, but I left before nine. Why do I feel awful?

MAN. (*Singing "MacArthur Park" offstage, sort of.*) "Someone left the cake out in the raaaain."

LYNNE. Mystery solved, I did it again.

MAN. "But I didn't want to take it. 'Cause it took so long to bake it ..."

LYNNE. I did it again.

MAN. (*Offstage.*) "And I'll never find that recipe agaaaaaiiiiinn. Ohhh, noooooooooo."

LYNNE. In the bathroom, taking a shower ... Hmmm? Wine, Drambuie, Creme de Menthe and, yes, I vomited. Let me check. (*Bends over side of bed; picks up size 84 shoe.*) He's tall. (*Puts finger through hole in heel of sock.*) Single. (*Picks up shirt.*) No convention tag, that's a good sign. And I better not bend over anymore. (*Leans back hard; feels a bump. Finds a coin changer under pillow; stares at changer.*) Oh, sweet Mother of Mary, it's a paperboy ... I don't remember, I don't remember, I do remember. It's the tax driver. I drove the cab, he rode in the back. Then we frolicked in Central Park ... It was safe. It was safe, he had a gun ... (*Beat.*) Whaddya mean, why do I do it? I need a hug. (*Mutters.*) Yah, well, needing sex seems more adult. (*Louder.*) I said, "needing sex seems more adult." I gotta get off the phone, I'm out of cigarettes. Because, I can't talk without a cigarette. I'm not kidding, I can't. (*Dawn.*) Oh God, I called Australia. I hope they weren't home.

MAN. (*Yells offstage.*) They were home!

LYNNE. They were home. Forgive me, I gotta get off the phone. (*Hangs up; crawls beneath sheets as LIGHTS fade-out.*)

MAN. (*Sings, offstage.*) "Ohhhh, nooooooooo."

(*Strains of "Auld Lang Syne." Fade-up on same bed. LIGHT streams from the fourth-wall window. A bedspread and sheet are carelessly covering the vitals of two lumps. The PHONE rings, a beefy male arm reaches out from the foot of the bed, blindly feeling for phone; the other lump extends a feminine arm. The fairer arm wins, taking the phone under the cover. As MUSIC fades, ANNOUNCER blends in with: "1979! HAPPY NEW YEAR, EVERYBODY!"*)

ELLIS. (*Moans.*) Hello ... (*Sits straight up; wearing her sheet.*) Oh hi, Aunt Grace, Happy Ne ... No, I'm awake ... Really ... Huh? (*Picks up* train schedule *from bedside table. Reads.*) "The Shoreliner 9:15; arrives Barnegat Bay 11:05." What time is it? ... You're right, I'm not on it. And you're all at the station? Oh hi, Mom, Happy N... I know, I'm not on it. What ti ... Uh huh ... What t ...

(*Quickly.*) What time's dinner? Oy. (*Starts to get up.*) Ham'll be fine ... I'll talk to her when I get there, okay? ... I didn't meet Guy Lombardo. I'll talk to her wh. Oh, hi, Mrs. Kepler ... I didn't meet Guy Lombardo. We were shooting in Times Square, he was at the Waldorf. Could we t ... Ham'll be fine (*Goes to hang up.*) I'll talk t ... Right. (*Hangs up. Swaddles in sheet and trundles out.*) Jim, wake up. Jim! (*Offstage.*) Why do I smell donuts? There's not much in the fridge. I didn't expect company or I'd've stocked the larder. Anyway, help yourself, I'm on a diet. (*Returns to room partially dressed. Hurriedly puts on* ring *from bedside table.*) Why do I smell donuts? (*Struggles with* earring.) I don't have a hangover. (*Beat.*) I'm manifesting a hangover to punish myself. (*One earring on.*) Would you pick up my check when you get yours? Why do I taste donuts? (*Exits rapidly. Enters in fury, throws donut box on bed.*) We ate donuts! (*Even louder.*) Four weeks, four lousy pounds and we ate donuts! (*Sits on bed; attempts other* earring.) Oh God, I can't afford people. I drink. I eat. I miss trains. Now I'm on sugar. (*Struggles with* earring.) I'm not on sugar. It's within my power. (*Still struggling with* earring.) "If a man is an inebriate convince the wrongdoer there is no real pleasure in false appetite." (*Drops earring on floor.*) Shit. (*Gets down on hands and knees looking under bed.*) Shit! (*Slumps against side of bed.*) Why do I have the feeling everything that happens today, and everybody I see, will punish me for being cranky?

(*CROSS-FADE as ELLIS and JIM exit. LYNNE walks casually into the neutral playing area with a bathroom scale under her arm like a notebook. SHE addresses the audience.*)

LYNNE. For the record, we had loftier goals than that, we really did. (*Beat.*) Every Monday, we'd embroider our brains with bumper stickers: "Happiness is Being Good." Every Saturday, we'd end up with a hangover, a man over, and the early morning regrets. Did you know baby chicks peck 10,000 times to get outta the shell? Can anyone tell me why? (*Beat.*) Some would argue, "You'll die if you stay in the shell." (*Sets down scale.*) Well, that's what I'm here to tell ya.

(*ELLIS enters with journal; steps on scale, impervious to LYNNE.*)

ELLIS. (*To herself.*) Four. I gained four. (*Steps off scale; sits on floor; writes in journal.*) For breakfast: one egg, small juice. For lunch: Scotch Broth soup.

(*LYNNE picks up scale and exits.*)

ELLIS. (*A confirmed soliloquizer—one-quarter to her journal; three-quarters to herself—ELLIS speaks with energy and determination, laughing throughout. The more apocalyptic; the more SHE laughs. Even the derision lacks self-pity.*) I got back from the Shore on Sunday, loaded down with New Year's resolutions: no eating, no drinking, go to gym, go to yoga. By Friday, I was sitting next to a buffet in Philadelphia, stuffing myself with stuffed grape leaves. I like sitting next to the food; gives me something to do with my hands. Saturday, we shot all day. For breakfast: one egg; small juice. For lunch: split pea soup. At dinner, my roast beef was an ounce over, but there wasn't much choice—or I didn't recognize the choice. Then I mini-binged on Melba Toast. I'd have gone to bed and avoided it if I hadn't been waiting for Glenn to call. (*Has stopped writing.*) Sunday was wonderful. We were together the whole day. That evening, I had a cheeseburger, two glasses of wine, and a six-pack of cottage cheese. (*Writes.*) On the train, I ate yogurt and stuffed in a Fresca. At home, things were frozen so I settled for crackers. It's lucky I got tired or I would have fried flour. I don't know what's bothering me. I don't want to cause trauma to Glenn's wife and children. I don't want to feel like a bad person again. I'd like to move someplace where I don't know anyone. Start all over. (*Laughs.*) But then I'd just end up being me. And have to move again. I'm probably just angry because I gained four lousy pounds. (*LIGHTS fade, along with voice.*) Starting Monday, I'll go to gym, go to yoga, and follow my eating plan religiously whether I like myself or not. I may make exceptions for extenuating circumstances but I won't create the extenuating circumstances. I must control my compulsiveness. Signed Ellis Crowley. (*Beat.*) I need to take a long cruise to Katmandu.

(*BLAST of an ocean liner; SOUND of ship's orchestra wafting through the night playing German "oom-pa-pa" version of "Auld Lang Syne." BAND MEMBER (offstage) yells above the music: 1980! HAPPY NEW YEAR, EVERYBODY!" LIGHTS up on bench area as LYNNE enters carrying sketch pads, knapsack, and a blanket. SHE sits on the bench that is now representing a deck chair, blankets her lap, and begins to sketch. ONE GERMAN and ANOTHER GERMAN enter, martini in hand, wearing "1980" New Year's glitter hats. As THEY look over Lynne's shoulder, SHE sketches faster. Silence.*)

ONE GERMAN. Illustrahtor?
LYNNE. (*Smiles shyly.*) Ja.
ONE GERMAN. Kinderbüchen?
LYNNE. Hmm?

ANOTHER GERMAN. Kin-der-büch-en?
LYNNE. No Sprechen so hot.
ONE GERMAN. Sprechen Sie kein Deutsch?
LYNNE. Un poquito.
ANOTHER GERMAN. (*Laughs.*) Un poquito.

(*GERMANS cross out of light to* boat railing, *still laughing.*)

LYNNE. (*To audience.*) Un poquito. Wonderful. I was invited to a Book Fair in Bremerhaven. I decided to take a slow boat because I wanted to be alone. I also thought I'd straighten out my life: no drinking, no smoking. I'd been on that boat three days. Greek Line out of New York. Everyone spoke German. Boy, was I alone. (*Pulls a blanket up tightly.*) And riddled with insomnia. A direct result, I suppose, of going to bed every night at eight. Can people die from lack of touch? (*Returns to sketching.*)

ELLIS. (*Enters USL; carrying knapsack, crosses to* deck chair.) Besetzt? [Occupied]
LYNNE. (*Guesses.*) Nein.
ELLIS. Danke.

(*Sits on bench. LYNNE burrows into sketching. ELLIS points to Lynne's sketch book. LYNNE burrows further.*)

ELLIS. Illustrahtor?
LYNNE. Ja.
ELLIS. Kinderbüchen?
LYNNE. Ja. Kinderbüchen.

(*BOTH smile; awkward.*)

ELLIS. Wo kommen Sie her? [Where are you from?]

LYNNE. Hmm?
ELLIS. Wo kommen Sie her? Verstehen Sie?
LYNNE. Nein, verstehen Sie. Amerikaner.
ELLIS. Amerikaner?
LYNNE. Ja.
ELLIS. Amerikaner, allzu.
LYNNE. Amerikaner, allzu?
ELLIS. Ja.
LYNNE. Ja? Then why are we talking like this?
ELLIS. I don't know.

(*Laughter from GERMANS; ANOTHER GERMAN mockingly mutters "Un poquito." ELLIS and LYNNE gaze enviously at the Germans' drinks. Long silence.*)

LYNNE. I want a drink so bad.
ELLIS. Have one.
LYNNE. No, thanks. I'd rather wake up alone tomorrow morning.
ELLIS. I know the feeling.

(*THEY continue to stare at drinks. Long silence.*)

LYNNE. I want a drink so bad.
ELLIS. I know the feeling.

(*BOTH watch as GERMANS exit laughing. Long, uncomfortable silence.*)

LYNNE. Oh God, I know it's my turn but I'm lousy at small talk. Did you see tonight's movie?
ELLIS. I hate "Benjy" movies.
LYNNE. Did you see last night's movie?
ELLIS. (*Matter of fact, rapidly.*) Benjy's gonna get lost, right? He's gonna get attacked by wolves and lay there,

bleeding and whimpering—all alone—while people wander through the forest yelling, "Benjy, Benjy." Then he's gonna limp 4,000 miles, crossing freeways that look like the Indianapolis 500, until he gets home and everybody's so glad to see him, they cry. Why should I put myself though that?

LYNNE. (*Looks at Ellis, then looks directly at audience. Beat.*) I should have known then, right? (*To Ellis.*) Oh, hell, let's have a drink? Want a drink?

ELLIS. No. (*Beat.*) And neither do you.

(*LIGHTING change. SOUND: Guy Lombardo's* Happy Days are Here Again *or Bette Midler blasts in: "But you've got to have friends./The feeling's oh so strong./You got to have friends./To make that day last long."* SOUND of thunder; SOUND OF rain. LYNNE and ELLIS on bench, huddled in blankets, sketch pads in laps, box of 48* Crayola's *by Lynne's side. BOTH are coloring.*)

ELLIS. Pass the mauve magenta.
LYNNE. There's no such thing as mauve magenta.
ELLIS. Pity. What else ya got?
LYNNE. Maize. Thistle. Bittersweet.
ELLIS. Thistle.
LYNNE. (*Hands Ellis* "thistle;" *colors.*) I'm so weak from lack of cigarettes, I can hardly color.
ELLIS. We can get a car when we dock at Le Havre. Cheap.

---

* Mention is made of songs which are *not* in the public domain. Producers of this play are hereby CAUTIONED that permission to produce this play does not include rights to use these songs in production. Producers should contact the copyright owners directly for rights.

LYNNE. How cheap?

ELLIS. Doesn't have reverse; doesn't have a rear-view mirror.

LYNNE. Doesn't have reverse; doesn't need a rear-view mirror. You drive, okay?

ELLIS. Oh, c'mon. What are you afraid of?

LYNNE. People, life, parallel parking. When I grow up, I want to be like Mrs. Minnock [min-knock] (*In harsh Brooklynese.*) "Can we have more strudel over here, honey?" (*Beat.*) She's getting to you, isn't she?

ELLIS. Not at all.

LYNNE. She got to you at breakfast.

ELLIS. Maybe to you; not to me.

LYNNE. Then why were you eating two donuts?

ELLIS. I wasn't eating two donuts.

LYNNE. You were, too. You had one in each hand.

ELLIS. I was?

LYNNE. Must be nice to be able to turn off your brain. I think about everything I ever did, and why I did it. Then, I analyze everybody else. (*Beat.*) Have you noticed depression's easier to handle than euphoria?

ELLIS. (*Crosses a page out.*) Yuck.

LYNNE. That's the fifth page you've started.

ELLIS. I'm into perfect. Pass the "burnt sienna."

(*LYNNE does.*)

ELLIS. It's broken.

LYNNE. Still colors.

ELLIS. (*Hands it back.*) I don't want it. It's broken. (*Takes another crayon; back to coloring.*) My world; I make the rules.

(*LYNNE checks Ellis for any sign of humor but ELLIS proceeds to color, feverishly.*)

LYNNE. I think we might be dealing with a serious character defect.

ELLIS. And plenty more where that came from.

(*LIGHTING change. SOUND: "I've got some friends but they're gaw-awn./Someone came and took them away."* * *BOTH rise and exit during music. ELLIS enters DSR, walking briskly. LYNNE follows.*)

ELLIS. You like picnics?
LYNNE. I love picnics.
ELLIS. Good, we'll go on picnics. You like boardwalks?
LYNNE. I love boardwalks.
ELLIS. Good. We'll stroll boardwalks.
LYNNE. Boy, you walk fast.
ELLIS. Got to get A-Deck before it closes.

(*SOUND: "And from the dusk till the daw-awn./Here is where I'll stay ..." ELLIS enters DSL, walks rapidly; LYNNE follows.*)

ELLIS. You like sailboats?
LYNNE. I love sailboats.
ELLIS. Good. We'll take your car to my sailboat.
LYNNE. Where's it moored?

---

* Mention is made of songs which are *not* in the public domain. Producers of this play are hereby CAUTIONED that permission to produce this play does not include rights to use these songs in production. Producers should contact the copyright owners directly for rights.

ELLIS. Barnegat Bay, near my mother's. You like church?

LYNNE. It's been awhile.

ELLIS. On Sundays we can go to church. (*Hurries off SR. SOUND: 'Cause you got to have fri-ends. La la, la la, la la la la." ELLIS enters DSR.*)

(*LYNNE races in, just in time to speak her line.*)

ELLIS. You like tilt-a-whirls?
LYNNE. I vomit on tilt-a-whirls.
ELLIS. Good. We'll ride separate tilt-a-whirls.
LYNNE. You like cats?
ELLIS. I hate cats.
LYNNE. You do?

(*BOTH stop in their tracks.*)

ELLIS. You don't?
LYNNE. No.
ELLIS. Actually, I like cats. Cats just don't like me.
LYNNE. How do you know?
ELLIS. I had a kitten once. It attacked my ankles.
LYNNE. Kittens do that.
ELLIS. (*Well, I'll be damned.*) Oh. I thought it didn't like me. (*SOUND: Blast of ocean liner; runs to railing.*) Land Ho!

LYNNE. (*Joins her; looks down.*) Where are the drums? The canoes? The brown-skinned tahini's swimming to greet us?

ELLIS. This is Ireland.
LYNNE. Oh.
BOTH. (*Mutual bear hug.*) Ireland!
LYNNE. There's a lot to be said for the buddy system.

ELLIS. True. If you're swimming and a shark comes along, there's a fifty percent chance he'll eat your buddy.

LYNNE. (*Stops, looks directly at audience. Beat.*) I should have known then, right?

ELLIS. Ready to go?

LYNNE. But we just got here.

ELLIS. Got to get to C-Deck before it closes. (*Walks off DSR.*)

LYNNE. (*Begins to follow Ellis out; then circles abruptly and returns to face the audience.*) I could show you more Hollywood vignettes: the walk on the beach, the run in the sand, the bicycle built for two; but, suffice it to say, we became good friends. Probably because, through all our travels, we shared one basically profound belief: If we were taken hostage, no one ... would negotiate. (*Shyly.*) That was some hug, did you catch that hug? People of the same sex usually give A-frame hugs, sparing all vital parts. Or kisses that meet in the air. But that was *some* hug.

(*LIGHTS up on bed area. ELLIS enters with quilt, covers bed, lies down, and begins to write a TV treatment in her journal.*)

LYNNE. I liked the kid in Ellis. The skater in search of a smooth sidewalk. I think mine suffered crib death. I've always been a bit stiff; afraid to be seen having fun. Some ride roller coasters, some wait below, holding the coats. Now, there's a t-shirt if I ever heard one. (*Crosses to bed area; sits on floor.*) We got back from Europe on the 23rd and spent the next three weekends at her mother's apartment in Barnegat Bay. (*Pulls out scrapbook from underneath bed; opens it.*) And I never did make it to Bremerhaven. (*Points in scrapbook.*) Who's that?

ELLIS. Me. Galveston. When I was six.

LYNNE. Another Easter, another stunning dress. The only thing missing are the Mary Janes.

ELLIS. Mom said they were too much work. She'd have to keep Vaseline on them or they'd crack. (*Touches Lynne.*) Listen. (*Reads.*) "This nighttime series will run the gamut of comedy, tragedy, et cetera." First episode: "Jennifer McCarthy looked in the mirror and declared herself fat." (*Shakes head; erases.*) "Lindsay J. Lakin looked in the mirror and declared herself fat."

LYNNE. What happened to "eina kleina film Direktor?"

ELLIS. You *write* "Rocky"; you *direct* "Rocky."

LYNNE. All these pictures. You're never smiling.

ELLIS. I'm not? (*Fascinated.*) I'm not, am I? (*Beat.*) I didn't speak 'til I was five.

LYNNE. Jesus, who were you mad at?

ELLIS. Mom says I was born angry.

HELEN. (*Enters in robe and slippers. SHE is small, thin, deeply tanned, and subject to outbursts of childlike wonder.*) What do you kids want for Sunday dinner? Tuna noodle casserole or Malarkey stew? (*Flops prone at foot of bed.*) I could make a quiche. What about meatloaf? With french fried onion rings ...

LYNNE. I love meatloaf.

HELEN. I know, a pot roast! Now all I have to do is figure out breakfast. Sure hope you kids brought better weather this weekend. I feel so fat and swollen; I need some sun.

ELLIS. Mom's a firm believer: If you can't lose it, tan it.

HELEN. Oh, I love it when you're with Lynne! Then you're in a good mood. Then I'm in a good mood.

LYNNE. (*Points to scrapbook.*) Who's this?

ELLIS. Marlene Fronzak. She was voted Most Repulsive. You know the kind, all gums and teeth. I'd always get the same kind of ice cream she did, so she wouldn't ask for a lick. That's it! Marlene Fronzak looked in the mirror ...

HELEN. (*Jumps up.*) I know, croissants! With sweet creamery butter. That's it, croissants. (*Beat.*) Or would you rather have bagels?

LYNNE. We'll have what you have.

HELEN. Me? (*Laughs.*) You'd end up with half a grapefruit and dry "glutton" toast. Now all I have to do is figure out lunch. (*Exits; voice drifts off.*) What sounds good? Soup? Sandwich? I could make egg salad. Better yet, hamburgers with thick melted cheese ...

(*A scrutable silence. LYNNE studies Ellis.*)

LYNNE. What are you thinking?

ELLIS. I don't know.

LYNNE. You really don't know, do you?

ELLIS. (*Leaps into lotus.*) Let's meditate. Want to meditate? Concentrate on the mantra, exclude all thoughts.

LYNNE. What are you meditating?

ELLIS. I'm thinking about the Sara Lee Cheesecake I'm not going to eat.

LYNNE. That's not what you're thinking.

ELLIS. Then why don't you tell me? You always do.

LYNNE. You're angry.

ELLIS. No, I'm not.

LYNNE. You're furious.

ELLIS. She's always talking about food. Why should I be angry about that? (*Thinks about it; amazed.*) You know, you're right. (*Furious.*) Boy, am I pissed. (*Gets up.*) I'm gonna get a donut. Want a donut?

LYNNE. No. (*Beat.*) And neither do you.

(*SOUND of congregation in full chorus: "Praise God, from Whom all Blessing Flows." THEY cross to area*

LIGHTING; raise hymnals. *ELLIS sings; LYNNE tears up. ELLIS hands Lynne a Kleenex.)*

LYNNE. *(To audience.)* One sang; the other was sobbing into her hymnal over lost youth. *(Closes hymnal; crosses to DS apron as LIGHTS fade on ELLIS.)* I gotta tell ya, it was more than I could bear. All that clean living: the sky cobalt blue, the sun, cadmium #4, tiny little ions scrubbing my soul; no booze, no cigarettes, no taxi drivers; and, on top of all that, *church.* I gotta tell ya ... *(Breathes in the sea air.)* The sun felt wonderful, the heat felt wonderful, even the Jersey flies felt wonderful.

(ELLIS enters, carrying a knapsack, sits on apron, DSL. SOUND: of surf and gulls.)

LYNNE. After church, we'd head for Island Beach—a long peninsula jutting into the Atlantic with mile after mile of sand. Ellis walked there in winter to sort things out. Her ritual became our ritual. We'd drive to the last parking bay, then walk the three miles to Barnegat Bay inlet, meeting no one. *(Crosses to Ellis.)* We were quite a team, I was always concentrating on the path below; she was always looking ahead, on the way to getting there. I don't think either of us ever saw the view. And I, of course, preferred to follow, preferred anyone's destination to my own. *(Sits next to Ellis.)* We'd sit on a large piece of driftwood, staring into the wind. We didn't talk much; we didn't need to. *(Rummages through knapsack; gets out baggie of trail mix.)* Obviously, we'd become very close. *(Takes a piece out.)* Probably, too close. *(Starts to put in mouth.)*

ELLIS. Oh, did I tell you? I'm moving to L.A.
LYNNE. Pardon me?

ELLIS. There's a possible shoot. Paramount. Not directing, but it'd be a foot in the door.

(*LYNNE returns piece to trail mix.*)

ELLIS. I feel so good about myself, lately. I've changed; I know I have, and if I don't move now, I never will. I won't allow any negative suggestion that failure is possible. Even if the Director's Guild goes on strike. Starting Monday, I'll phone Roger Corman, Orion, revise my resume, and just plain start over.

(*LYNNE has returned trail mix to knapsack; has pulled out address book and is thumbing through it.*)

ELLIS. You gonna call someone?
LYNNE. I just thought I'd read my address book. It's been a long time.
ELLIS. Who knows, I'll probably be making enough in a year to afford a house. Especially if I'm directing. I *will* be directing. (*Silence. Gets up; brushes sand off.*) Ready to go.
LYNNE. Yep.

(*ELLIS crosses, turns to see if Lynne is behind her. No Lynne. Exits. Silence.*)

LYNNE. (*To audience.*) We'd made it through fifty-one days, but that's not a record. In August, 1837, Patricia Bingham of Bayonne, New Jersey, traveled with her friend, Cicely Tubb, for fifty-three days before they jumped into the Watanabee [Wa-tah-nah-bee] River. Their hands around each other's throats. (*Beat.*) Actually, I like being alone. I think my mother left me a lot when I was little. I only want to be alone or with people I love. Everybody else feels like babysitters. (*Rises; dusts herself off.*) It really is a lovely day. (*Points.*) One of the last sailboats of autumn just entered Barnegat Bay.

(*Exits. LIGHTING change as PHONE rings once. HELEN enters, sits on bench, sunbathing in sleeveless top. Another RING, LIGHTS up on ELLIS pacing near bed with phone, speaks energetically. HELEN listens as if in reverie.*)

ELLIS. Mom, L.A. is great! I'm directing a soap! Twice a week, an hour soap! (*Puts down phone; lifts up phone; PHONE rings once.*) Mom, L.A. is great! I bought a house! It needs a little work, but I bought a house. (*Puts down phone; lifts up phone; PHONE rings once.*) Mom, L.A. is great! I met a man! He needs a little work, but I met a man.

(*Puts down phone; lifts up phone; PHONE rings once. LIGHTS out on HELEN; LIGHTS up on LYNNE in neutral area—smoking a cigarette, sans phone.*)

ELLIS. Lynne, L.A. is great! I got a soap, I bought a house, I met a man. (*Laughs; reverse quilt for L.A. change.*) Sometimes he becomes the enemy for liking me but he's terrific. So's the house. And I found a doctor who believes in allergy diets. And a psychiatrist, Ardis Baker— you know the one, on all the talk shows. She said she'd take me on but I'd have to be better in six months because she's got a new book and a national tour. So, I'll just skip my childhood and get to the good stuff. (*LIGHTS out on ELLIS.*)

LYNNE. Signed Ellis Crowley. (*LIGHTS up on bed area as LYNNE crosses through.*) Ellis lept from platitude to platitude across a shallow brook—until she came to deep water. (*SOUND: "Auld Lang Syne."*) 1981. Happy New Year. (*Exits.*)

ELLIS. (*Crawls under L.A. quilt, grocery bag on floor, headphones on bedpost. SUN trying to peek through drawn shades. Writes in journal. Stops. Thinks aloud. Voice is a little less energetic.*) I was sick again all weekend. There's a thousand things I should be doing, like working on this house. I thought I'd earn enough to fix it, but I got fired. Well, not fired. They didn't renew my contract. It felt like fired. It was fired. (*Beat.*) I set out to prove I was a good director; all I proved was the need for perfection and two shows a week make you tired. And every month there'd be this pain. The crew'd have coffee breaks, I'd have vomit breaks. I didn't dare tell them. It's so hard for women to break into television, and cramps is such a lame excuse. Wednesday, I had spearmint tea, two Naprosyn, and an Alka Seltzer Plus. I'd like to call Lynne, but I don't dare. People get to know me, then walk away. Or did I walk away? (*Grabs stomach.*) Maybe I'm depressed about this hysterectomy business. I went to one of the best doctors in Beverly Hills five months ago. She said it was all in my head. Now, this doctor says fibroids. "My body and my brain are my servants not my master." (*Beat.*) Thursday, I had three ounces of veal, four ounces of spinach, and a brief affair. Why does going to bed with someone you don't even care about hurt so much when they don't call after? I guess I feel he didn't respect me. I guess I didn't respect myself. I guess I don't trust men. (*Beat.*) I'd like to call Lynne, but I don't dare. When you start to depend on someone, you give away too much power. Mom is so needy—I don't want to be like that. You can't depend on anyone ever. It's as simple as that. (*Laughs.*) I guess I don't trust women. (*Beat.*) Starting Monday, I'm going to run five miles around the lake whether I have cramps or not; mail ten resumes instead of five; call eight people instead of four; go to Paramount, go to Warner's. Signed Ellis Crowley. I can't keep calling Lynne.

(*Puts on headphones from bedpost. SOUND of "Fame"* *
bumps in mid-tape: "Baby, look at me ..." Burrows under covers. LYNNE enters on "I'll make you forget the rest," crosses to bed; lifts off headphones.)

LYNNE. Say anything you want, okay? Just don't be polite.
ELLIS. What are you doing here?
LYNNE. That's too polite.
ELLIS. What are you doing here, Fuckface?
LYNNE. (*To audience.*) She didn't say that. And I didn't just show up. Truth be told: she started to phone—once in November, twice in December—laughing so high, I could hear the lows. (*To Ellis.*) Jesus, this house is colder than Minnesota.
ELLIS. There's no heat.
LYNNE. (*Looks around.*) Furniture?
ELLIS. (*Abrupt energy change.*) One card table, one chair, one couch, one bed. But it really is a good investment. It's right near Carroll Avenue, where they have those large Victorian houses. Want to see? (*Walks a few feet, UL. LYNNE follows.*) Voila. Living room.
LYNNE. (*A pathetic "ooh;" a delayed:*) Nice, really nice.
ELLIS. The speckled mirrors aren't staying.

---

* Mention is made of songs which are *not* in the public domain. Producers of this play are hereby CAUTIONED that permission to produce this play does not include rights to use these songs in production. Producers should contact the copyright owners directly for rights.

LYNNE. What about the bamboo wallpaper?
ELLIS. Not staying. The fireplace, however, is. (*Walks UC; LYNNE follows.*) Kitchen avec pantry.
LYNNE. Nice. Really nice. (*Beat*.) And blue. Really blue.
ELLIS. (*Walks UL; LYNNE follows.*) Bathroom.
LYNNE. Nice. Nice spirit. Where are the walls?
ELLIS. I tore them down. (*Walks a few feet, UR.*) Den.

(*LYNNE emits an anemic "ah;" a delayed "ni ..." ELLIS continue hastily to bed area.*)

ELLIS. My bedroom.

(*LYNNE looks in; silence.*)

ELLIS. I have to admit, it needs a little facelift.

(*LYNNE is stunned.*)

ELLIS. But it really is Victorian.

(*LYNNE is more than stunned.*)

ELLIS. Like Mrs. Sutphen's [Sut-fens]. Remember Mrs. Sutphen's ...

(*LYNNE wants to go home.*)

ELLIS. On the road to the shore ... (*Silence.*) This house could look as nice. (*Silence.*) Whaddya think?
LYNNE. Excuse me. (*Rushes to audience; words pour out.*) How could I tell her it looked like a whorehouse? I was swallowing eight lines per: Den of what? Thieves? Opium? Needs a little facelift. Needs a little forklift. Who

did the color scheme, Shanghai Lil? There were holes in every wall. I don't mean nail holes ... (*Holds out arms.*) I mean holes. And her bedroom. Her bedroom. Was the ugliest color I'd ever seen. No wonder she was depressed. It looked like a whorehouse.

(*Returns reluctantly. BOTH continue to gaze at room in silence. Finally:*)

ELLIS. Whaddya think? Like the color? (*Silence.*) I call it: Puke green. God, it's good to see you. (*Bear hugs Lynne. LYNNE looks at audience.*)

LYNNE. What about upstairs?

ELLIS. (*Points to offstage steps.*) Feel free.

LYNNE. Aren't you coming? (*Exits.*)

ELLIS. I'd rather not. (*ELLIS rushes to bedroom; gets grocery bag from side of bed; looks for hiding place. Yells as SHE goes.*) I've been going to paint. But I'm terrified I'll choose the wrong paint. Well, would I change in one year? The roof leaks, it's in the worst crime district in L.A., the back door's paper thin, and I'm still living out of suitcases.

LYNNE. (*Offstage.*) Ellis! This *was* a whorehouse! There are nude women wallpapering the walls in every conceivable position. (*Hurries in aghast; same voice pitch.*) Some not so conceivable. This *was* a whorehouse!

ELLIS. Why do you think it was so cheap?

LYNNE. Doesn't it bother you?

ELLIS. Not if I don't think about it.

LYNNE. What's in the bag?

ELLIS. (*Rummages in grocery bag.*) Sara Lee Danish, donuts assorted, Mint Milanos, and a Peter Paul Mound.

LYNNE. (*Takes bag; rolls down top.*) Look. Want to do something tomorrow? Scripps Museum? Venice Beach?

"Let's Make a Deal"? We could win a refrigerator or boat for your house.

ELLIS. I can't.

LYNNE. What about Friday?

ELLIS. I can't.

LYNNE. Booked, eh?

ELLIS. Sort of.

LYNNE. (*Goes to door.*) Well, hey, I've kept you long enough. The house is wonderful, the windows are wonderful, the fireplace is wonderful, the vestibule's wonderful and I'm gonna keep invoking "wonderfuls" as I back out the door, hoping I can get out of here with my dignity intact and not all over your kitchen floor.

ELLIS. I'm glad you came.

LYNNE. Yah, same. (*Turns to exit.*)

ELLIS. I have to go to the hospital tomorrow.

LYNNE. Who's sick?

ELLIS. Me. Hysterectomy. Just partial, nothing serious.

LYNNE. Who's taking you?

ELLIS. Me.

LYNNE. You're going alone?

ELLIS. Is that odd?

LYNNE. What time should I pick you up?

ELLIS. It's okay.

LYNNE. I know it's okay. What time should I pick you up?

ELLIS. Is ten too early?

LYNNE. Ten's just fine. (*Turns to go.*)

ELLIS. Where are you staying?

LYNNE. A motel on Sunset.

ELLIS. Want to stay here?

(*As LIGHTS fade, there is a swirl of activity. NURSE and MALE NURSE enter and add white sheet to bedding, position chair away from the bed as ELLIS gets into it. DOCTOR enters neutral area in surgery garb, stands with back to audience. AREA LIGHTING as LYNNE approaches him and converses quietly. SHE addresses audience with no emotion.)*

LYNNE. He told me there were complications, the fibroids weren't fibroids. He told me she had cancer; he hoped it hadn't spread. (*DOCTOR exits.*) That's all I remember. That and his pocket. To this day, I can remember every detail of his pocket: light green institutional stitching, one thread hanging out. And a pen, a small black felt tip, a white dot on its crown. I remember wondering if the pocket would break my fall. It was the only thing to grab on to; except for the words hanging in the air. (*Crosses to "hospital" bed.*)

(*ELLIS is sleeping lightly. ELLIS wakes, incapable of movement.*)

LYNNE. Hi.
ELLIS. Hi.
LYNNE. How are you feeling?
ELLIS. Pummeled. I keep thinking I've done something wrong.
LYNNE. Your mother should be here any minute. Her plane got in at four.
ELLIS. I wish you hadn't done that.
LYNNE. My God, she had to know.
ELLIS. I really wish you hadn't done that.
LYNNE. Why?
HELEN. (*Crashes in, carrying suitcase.*) I am so exhausted! (*Plots in chair.*) I don't know why I'm so exhausted, but I am. I'm just exhausted!
ELLIS. (*Gently; unable to see her.*) Mom.

HELEN. (*Staring at floor; trembling.*) I feel so fat and swollen ... could be the ham. I drank gallons of water all night last night; got up this morning and weighed five more pounds.

ELLIS. Mom.

HELEN. (*Relates to no one.*) Either that or the diuretic. I should know better than to take a diuretic when I'm flying; but I took a diuretic. I am absolutely exhausted.

ELLIS. (*Softly; as to a child.*) Would you like Lynne to take you to the house?

HELEN. Could she?

LYNNE. Now?

HELEN. (*Crosses to neutral area as voice drifts off in the dark.*) If I could just get some potassium. That's all that's wrong: potassium. If I could just lie down ...

(*CROSS-FADE as NURSE enters and helps ELLIS exit, striking sheet. LYNNE walks into bench area, addressing audience.*)

LYNNE. She really did that; I didn't make it up. (*Admits reluctantly.*) Okay the Germans and the cruise I made up. But that's all I made up. She *really* did that. And I *really* judged her. By some vague motherhood measuring stick. She wasn't too strong in the best of times and now she was reeling.

(*LIGHTS up, neutral area. HELEN is sitting on suitcase, staring at floor, despondent.*)

LYNNE. (*Grabs bucket from behind bench and crosses to her.*) You take the bed, I'll take the couch. (*Beat.*) I want to fix up her room. Paint, plug up the holes, get curtains. (*Beat.*) What time do you want to go to the hospital in the morning?

HELEN. I just need a day or two to rest.

LYNNE. You're not going to the hospital?

HELEN. Just a day or two.

LYNNE. (*Gently.*) You're burying her, you know. You've got the shovel and you're burying her.

HELEN. (*Becomes Lynne's child.*) What do you want me to do?

LYNNE. Wanna grab a brush?

(*HELEN takes bucket.*)

LYNNE. (*Addresses audience.*) By God, she did. And we painted four rooms.

(*HELEN dips brush into bucket, paints.*)

LYNNE. The biopsies were good news: the cancer hadn't spread. The doctors decided on an aggressive approach: chemo and radiation. I convinced Ellis that people with pets live longer. So she got a kitten, pronounced him "Holbein [Hole-bine]." Got a dog, pronounced her "Grace." Grace was part German shepherd, part timberwolf.

HELEN. (*Looks back at her handiwork.*) Oh, she's gonna love this room.

LYNNE. (*To audience.*) Neither of us had ever lived with anyone; so we both had a long way to go. Ellis had trouble if the shower curtain was left the wrong way. And I reflected her every mood. If she had a bad day, I had a bad day. I asked her once, in the middle of our weekly fight, what she was getting out of this. She said, "I'm no longer lonely."

HELEN. (*Stands up, stiff with arthritis.*) She's gonna love this room.

LYNNE. We worked hard on the house: bought used furniture; scraped off nudes; I started a book; we didn't drink. Ellis sent out resumes; lost her hair; directed a sitcom; her hair grew back; we didn't drink. I loved her hair.

(*HELEN exits with suitcase and paint.*)

LYNNE. We became quite a family. Nestled in on Sunday mornings, reading the *New York Times*. I'd always wanted an "old shoe" relationship. You know, like Dagwood and Blondie, reading newspapers in an overstuffed living room, twin floor lamps. We sort of had that. (*Beat.*) I've always loved indiscriminately: men, women, families, dogs, Blackwing Pencils. Truth be told: I have sex with men; no love. Love with women; no sex. I don't think there's a name for me yet. (*Beat.*) Two months later, her mother went home. Eight months later, I went home. And Ellis got a clean bill of health.

(*LIGHTS up on bench area which is now a large waiting area in the hospital, Houston. SOUND: of TV-movie. ELLIS enters, carrying a pen and her journal; sits on bench. TRISH wheels in a PATIENT IN WHEELCHAIR, dazed and extremely thin, parks him/her nearby. TRISH exits. ELLIS and PATIENT IN WHEELCHAIR stare up at an unseen television screen.*)

LYNNE. Then one day in August an x-ray resurfaced, filed away by mistake. They held it up so she could see the smudges on the lungs. They said to go to Houston. The cancer center there. They'd do more tests in Houston. Then tell us what was up. (*Joins Ellis, SOUND fades down.*)
ELLIS. Ask them how much longer.

LYNNE. But we just got here.

ELLIS. Our appointment was at eight, right? It's eight-o-two.

LYNNE. Shouldn't we give it a reasonable length of time?

ELLIS. Today, two minutes is reasonable. My world; I make the rules. I wish they'd turn off this movie.

LYNNE. What is it?

ELLIS. *Death Be Not Proud.*

LYNNE. Jesus.

ELLIS. Can you change the channel? (*Beat.*) Well?

LYNNE. (*Amazed. Looks around.*) I can't just change the channel!

ELLIS. Why not?

LYNNE. *Everybody in this room* is watching it. (*Slumps.*)

(*NURSE EATON enters SL, looks directly at Ellis, looks down at clipboard.*)

ELLIS. (*Braces.*) No chemo. I don't care what they say. If I've only got two years to live, I don't want to live it over a toilet bowl.

NURSE EATON. Mrs. Sternlicht. Mrs. Trudi Sternlicht.

ELLIS. (*Unbraces.*) We're going to miss our plane.

LYNNE. It doesn't leave 'til four. We've got eight hours.

(*SOUND out. NURSE EATON exits, SR. LIGHTING change to suggest passage of time. ELLIS jots down notes in journal. SOUND: Theme song from "The Young and the Restless." Sound fades out. ELLIS itches ankle.*)

ELLIS. Ask them how much longer.
LYNNE. I've asked a hundred times.
ELLIS. You afraid to ask?
LYNNE. Yes.
ELLIS. I'll ask.

(*NURSE EATON enters SR and walks to Patient in Wheelchair.*)

ELLIS. (*Sweetly.*) Excuse me.
NURSE EATON. (*Merry singsong as SHE exits with PATIENT IN WHEELCHAIR.*) Shouldn't be long.
ELLIS. I want to punish them. I really do. I won't tell them about anything that hurts.
LYNNE. Good, Ellis.
ELLIS. We're going to miss our plane.
LYNNE. It doesn't leave 'til four. We've got six hours.

(*LIGHTING change. SOUND: "Like sands in the hourglass, so are the 'Days of Our Lives.'" LYNNE exits ELLIS is writing in journal as MRS. KOENIG enters and sits next to her. ELLIS looks up—too late to say anything. SOUND fades as LYNNE returns; stands next to Ellis.*)

LYNNE. They say we're next.
ELLIS. Ask them what "next" means.
LYNNE. They're getting annoyed.
ELLIS. How annoyed?
LYNNE. Maybe not annoyed, maybe ... remote.
ELLIS. Then why did you say "annoyed"?
LYNNE. I got carried away.
TRISH. (*Enters SR.*) Mrs. Koenig [kay-nig]. Mrs. Doris Koenig. (*Exits with MRS. KOENIG, SL.*)
ELLIS. But she just got here!

LYNNE. Maybe she's seeing a different doctor.
ELLIS. Maybe she's seeing a faster doctor.
LYNNE. (*Sits next to Ellis.*) Maybe it's good yours is slow. Once you're in there, he might take his time.
ELLIS. I don't want him to take his time.
LYNNE. You want him to hurry?
ELLIS. (*Whispered frenzy.*) I want you to stop being rational!

(*LYNNE becomes riveted to TV as NURSE EATON enters SL.*)

NURSE EATON. Miss Howe. Miss Bobbie Howe. (*Exits SR.*)
ELLIS. (*With urgency.*) There's a scream coming up my throat.

(*LYNNE looks around; embarrassed.*)

ELLIS. I'm not kidding, keep talking. I'm not kidding, keep talking.
LYNNE. (*Talks fast.*) Okay, I'm talking. Hear me, I'm talking. Maybe they can't find your chart. Maybe they lost it; maybe ...
ELLIS. You mean the doctor can't see me until they find my chart!
LYNNE. I'm talking in "maybe's." I'm talking in "maybe's." Lunch! We need lunch. How 'bout some hot chicken soup? Peanut butter and jelly? Tuna on rye. I sound like your mother. How 'bout a luscious grilled cheese?
ELLIS. We're going to miss our plane.
LYNNE. We'll get one tomorrow.
ELLIS. They're booked for tomorrow.
LYNNE. We'll get one on Sunday.

ELLIS. And spend the weekend in Houston?
LYNNE. We'll go to the Houston Zoo.
ELLIS. Swell. Two horses and a cow.
LYNNE. That's not fair, it's an international zoo.
ELLIS. Two llamas and a cow.
NURSE EATON. (*Enters SL; exits SR.*) Mrs. McAllister. Darlyne McAllister.
TRISH. (*Enters SR; exits SL.*) Miss Jasper. Miss Barbara Jasper.
ELLIS. I'm not kidding, keep talking. I'm not kidding, keep talking.
LYNNE. We'll drive to Galveston.
ELLIS. Without a car?
LYNNE. We'll rent a car.
ELLIS. And where will we stay?
LYNNE. We'll rent a room. A beautiful room with a beautiful view.
ELLIS. Of what? A beautiful oil rig?
LYNNE. We'll walk on the beach.
ELLIS. And wade in the oil.
LYNNE. We'll swim in the ocean.
ELLIS. It has men-of-war.
LYNNE. You said you liked Galveston!
ELLIS. I changed my mind.
LYNNE. You're sure you want me to keep talking?
ELLIS. When I'm upset, I hate small talk. It just makes me more upset.
LYNNE. (*Screams; or keels slowly off bench onto floor. Holds position for a beat; gets up, and sits back on bench. To audience.*) That's what I wanted to do ... This is what I did. (*Turns to Ellis.*) Sure you don't want some lunch?
ELLIS. This is barbaric. (*Bolts off bench; exits SR.*)
LYNNE. (*Chases after her.*) Ellis! Ellis!

(CROSS-FADE as ELLIS enters SL; paces stage apron; LYNNE joins her.)

ELLIS. *(Whispered fury:)* You want me to be a good sport, don't you? They're gonna tell me how long I have to live and you want me to be a good sport. What if I decide not to get help, what if I decide to go home? No drugs, no treatments. And if I die in two years, I die.

LYNNE. Then I'll go with you. But I'll tell you something. You're going to sit in L.A. wanting to know. You will, Ellis. You'll spend every minute wanting to know. *(Beat.)* You're right, the waiting sucks. It's crap, it's shit, it's every toilet term I can think of. But you can't control it. You can't control the waiting, you can't control the doctors, you can't control anything.

ELLIS. Then what do I do?

LYNNE. Hand it over.

ELLIS. To what?

LYNNE. Believe me, there's a metaphysical Tootsie Pop somewhere at the end of this.

ELLIS. You know what my biggest fear is? Honest to God, my biggest fear.

LYNNE. What?

ELLIS. That I'll cry when they tell me.

LYNNE. My God, don't you think they've seen tears?

NURSE EATON. *(Offstage.)* Miss Crowley. Miss Ellis Crowley.

(CROSS-FADE as BOTH cross to neutral area which is now the examination room. NURSE EATON enters, sets down chair for Ellis. ELLIS sits, takes out journal, LYNNE addresses audience.)

LYNNE. Her moment of truth turned into another twenty minutes. *(To herself.)* I wonder if I should leave when the doctor comes? (*To Ellis.*) You think I should leave?

ELLIS. We're going to miss our plane.

LYNNE. I know. (*Beat.*) You think I should leave?

(*ELLIS braces as TRISH and DR. BENBERG hurry in. THEY do not, however, hurry the interview; nor do THEY have southern accents. BENBERG is wearing a large cowboy hat with what looks like a peacock feather.*)

TRISH. Good morning.

ELLIS. Good afternoon.

TRISH. Whatever.

BENBERG. How you feeling? (*Peruses file.*)

LYNNE. (*Steps out of scene; to audience.*) This really happened; I didn't make it up. Okay, okay, the Germans and the cruise I made up. But this *really* happened. There was Cougar madness in Houston. The team was in contention for the NCAA [NC Double A] title and half the hospital was in cowboy clothes. T-shirts with Phi Gamma Slamma or Phi Slamma Jamma. This *really* happened. (*Beat.*) But I don't think I want it to happen again. (*Takes off Benberg's hat.*) Excuse me. (*Walks hat to wings; returns.*)

BENBERG. How you feeling?

ELLIS. I have a sore throat. First time I've been sick in a year. (*Laughs.*) If you don't count cancer.

BENBERG. (*To Trish.*) I'm missing a scan.

(*TRISH exits.*)

BENBERG. I see you had adriamycin. (*Seems disappointed.*) Kind of conservative dose.

ELLIS. You going to increase it?

BENBERG. Can't. They gave you just enough to make you immune.

ELLIS. I see. (*Looks at journal. Throughout the following, her journal is her anchor.*) What about nutrition.

BENBERG. Only for slow growing cancers.

ELLIS. Mine's not so slow?

BENBERG. Not so slow.

ELLIS. (*Checks off list with pen.*) Interferon?

(*BENBERG shakes head "no."*)

ELLIS. (*Checks off list.*) Thermal?

BENBERG. Your best bet's another form of chemo.

ELLIS. I thought adriamycin was the best.

BENBERG. It was.

ELLIS. I see. (*Tries to control voice.*) What if I don't do anything? How long would I have?

BENBERG. (*Not harsh; straight forward.*) Without treatment? Six months.

ELLIS. (*Beat.*) With treatment?

BENBERG. Six months, maybe longer.

ELLIS. I see. (*Checks off list.*) How much longer?

BENBERG. Less than ten percent chance of complete remission for about two years.

ELLIS. I see. (*Checks off list.*) Quality of life?

BENBERG. If all goes well, you'll only be sick the last month.

ELLIS. (*Looks at journal.*) How will I die?

BENBERG. Malnutrition.

ELLIS. I see. (*Checks off list.*) What would *you* do?

BENBERG. If it were my life? Take the chemo; go for the odds. (*Beat.*) You'd be here two weeks. (*Hands blank paper to Ellis.*) And you'd have to sign this consent form.

(While ELLIS reads form, TRISH enters with report and clipboard. Subtly, but visibly thrown, SHE hands report to BENBERG. BENBERG reads it. HE, too, reacts.)

ELLIS. It says one of the side effects is heart damage. *(Laughs.)* I guess it doesn't matter.
BENBERG. *(Feels her shoulder.)* There's another small tumor in your shoulder. Feel it?
ELLIS. Yes.
BENBERG. Good. We can watch the cancer's growth with it. There are two tumors on the liver, one on the vertebrae. Not good.
ELLIS. Can things be worse?
BENBERG. Three months worse.
ELLIS. I just lost three months?
BENBERG. Yes.
ELLIS. I see.

(THEY wait for decision.)

ELLIS. *(Places a check in journal, laughs nervously.)* Guess I'd better take the chemo.
BENBERG & TRISH. Good!

(Laconic tone changes to urgent and personable. HE looks at Trish; SHE looks at clipboard.)

TRISH. EKG nine tomorrow. Subclavian at ten. The earliest I can get a cat scan is at Del Oro, a week from today.
ELLIS. A week? Eight weeks of quality time, three of them in Houston?
BENBERG. Could be worse, could be Lubbock. Can I see her tomorrow?

TRISH. You've got poor Mrs. Blane. What about tomorrow evening?

BENBERG. I've got poor Mr. Hoffman and poor Mr. Vogel.

TRISH. (*To Lynne and Ellis.*) Don't worry, we'll fit you in.

(*BENBERG rushes out; TRISH follows. Long silence.*)

ELLIS. Malnutrition? (*Explodes into laughter.*) Malnutrition! Did you get that statistic?

LYNNE. "Less than ten percent chance of complete remission for about two years."

ELLIS. Can you tell me what it means?

LYNNE. I was going to ask you.

ELLIS. Hell, I don't know.

LYNNE. You nodded like you knew.

ELLIS. I nod well.

LYNNE. You didn't know and you didn't ask?

ELLIS. Well, would I change in two minutes?

(*Roars; infectious; LYNNE joins in.*)

LYNNE. Maybe it means, "If you last two years, you're out of the woods."

ELLIS. Maybe it means, "There's less than ten percent of chance of lasting two years."

LYNNE. What about after two years?

ELLIS. (*Roars.*) Then everybody's dead. (*Laughs; stops abruptly.*) What's the date?

LYNNE. September 7th.

ELLIS. I'll be dead before Christmas. (*Flips pen in air; it sails behind her.*) I'm going to die in three months and I don't even have a headache.

LYNNE. You have a sore throat.

(This sends BOTH into high hysterics.)

ELLIS. *(Serious.)* I feel like I'm on some kind of journey.
LYNNE. Can I come along?
ELLIS. What? Share my death? You're asking a lot. I never shared my life.
LYNNE. I don't know what to say.
ELLIS. How 'bout, "Bye, bye?" *(Roars.)* Maybe I found my life's work. I die well. *(Roars.)* Malnutrition!

(LIGHTS come up on bench area. FARMER and FARMER'S WIFE enter carrying chairs and subclavian kits—clear plastic buckets containing a t-tube, an alcohol prep pad, a tubex, a heparin needle, and an opsite bandage. THEY place pamphlets under chairs. ELLIS gets up and crosses out of Lynne's light.)

ELLIS. *(Sits on bench; laughs again.)* Malnutrition?
LYNNE. *(Addresses audience as NURSE EATON enters with a lectern or tray containing a catheter, hemostat, and heparin needle and stands opposite class.)* The nurses were our lifeline. That one's name was Trish. There really was a Trish. *(Crosses stage.)* When the nurses were good, they were very very good. And when they were bad ...
NURSE EATON. *(Booms loudly.)* YOU ARE HERE...

(LYNNE rushes into scene, sliding timidly onto her bench seat.)

NURSE EATON. ... because you've had a catheter inserted into your subclavian area.
FARMER. Subclavian?
FARMER'S WIFE. Shoulder.

FARMER. Oh.

NURSE EATON. Because chemotherapy weakens veins—the subclavian catheter is your best friend. To administer chemo, the technician need only insert the IV into the heparin cap ...

(*FARMER raises hand.*)

NURSE EATON. I'll be happy to answer all questions at the end. (*Continues to demonstrate.*) ... and the liquid courses through the catheter into the blood stream. It is imperative the tube be kept clean, the line kept from clogging. Before you leave Houston, your "significant other" must demonstrate his ability to maintain it.

ELLIS. You mean I won't be able to take care of this myself?

NURSE EATON. (*Laughs.*) Hardly. (*Holds up heparin needle.*) This is heparin solution. It is used daily to flush the catheter. (*Like Houdini; rapid speed.*) Pick up your tubex. (*SHE holds it up.*)

(*ALL scramble to find the newly-named tubex.*)

NURSE EATON. Crack it ...

(*SHE does; THEY try.*)

NURSE EATON. ... insert the heparin needle and pull.

(*Voila. Class has only just begun. FARMER raises hand.*)

NURSE EATON. It is imperative, I repeat, imperative to rid the heparin solution of air bubbles.

(*FARMER'S WIFE raises hand.*)

NURSE EATON. If you do not, air will enter via the t-tube into the blood stream. You don't want air bubbles in your t-tube.
LYNNE. (*Raises hand, hesitantly.*) Uh ... what's a t-tube?
NURSE EATON. (*Singsong.*) Figure six, page four. Nor do you want water. Never—under any circumstances—get your catheter wet.
ELLIS. You mean I can't take a shower?
NURSE EATON. They didn't tell you?
ELLIS. No.
NURSE EATON. They should have. (*Holds needle up.*) To eject the air bubble, hold the needle straight up and push the plunger.
ELLIS. I can't take a shower!

(*LYNNE slumps in her seat.*)

NURSE EATON. You could have. With a peripheral catheter implanted in your arm.
ELLIS. You mean, I had a choice?
NURSE EATON. Certainly.

(*ELLIS drops tubex into bucket, sits with arms folded, staring.*)

NURSE EATON. Your catheter may be a little inconvenient, but I'm sure your veins will thank you. Hold the heparin needle between your fingers, open a prep pad, and clean off the heparin cap.

(*FARMER'S WIFE holds alcohol prep pad up for others. With needle between fingers, along with prep pad, class*

STARTING MONDAY

*has trouble grabbing hold of heparin cap to wipe it.
NURSE EATON has five hands.)*

NURSE EATON. Insert the needle into the heparin cap and gently push the plunger. If you meet any resistance, don't push or you'll blow a hole right out of your catheter.

(ALL hands shoot up, minus ELLIS.)

NURSE EATON. *(Perseveres.)* I repeat, if you hear a pop; run to a doctor. Give heparin shots the same time daily, change op-sites once a week.

(LYNNE fixes her hair with upraised hand.)

FARMER. Op-sites?
NURSE EATON. Figure twelve, page eight.

(In Rockette-like synchronation, ALL but ELLIS reach below chair for pamphlets.)

ELLIS. *(Loudly to Farmer.)* Did they tell you you couldn't take a shower?

(CLASS lowers eyes; LYNNE cleans off her shoe.)

FARMER. Hell, they don't tell you nothin'.
NURSE EATON. When you change the op-site, feel around the incision. Is it red? Is it swollen?

(ALL hands shoot up; all but ELLIS.)

LYNNE. Could we get back to the "pop"?

(Chorus of whispered "Yah's.")

NURSE EATON. Use a hemostat ...
ELLIS. What's a hemostat?
NURSE EATON. (*Holds up hemostat for Ellis to see.*) ... to avoid getting germs on the hub.
ELLIS. What's a hub?

(*LYNNE cleans off her other shoe.*)

NURSE EATON. Another name for a t-tube.
ELLIS. What's a t-tube? (*Singsongs with EATON.*) Figure six, page four. (*Beat.*) Can I turn this in on a peripheral?
NURSE EATON. If you want to wait a week.
ELLIS. That's all we do is wait.

(*ALL softly mutter; overlap.*)

ELLIS. We wait in insurance, we wait in pharmacy, we wait in blood and urine.
FARMER'S WIFE. They keep you waitin' 'til ya don't care if you live or die. Then they tell ya, when ya don't care.
FARMER. I'd wait a week, if I know'd it was a week. But their weeks is two weeks.

NURSE EATON. (*Seeking an ally; chooses Lynne.*) I'm sure the "waiting" causes frustration, but like I tell all my relatives, "If you're going to have cancer, *have* it in Houston." Patients have been known to make life-long friends in this hospital.
ELLIS. (*Rises.*) What's that? Three months? (*Storms off.*)

(NURSE EATON catches LYNNE's uncomfortable eye, smiles as if she were a confederate.)

NURSE EATON. *(To Lynne.)* She'll be back; she has no choice.

(LYNNE squirms; nailed eye to eye. As Eaton drones on, LYNNE slowly backs out of scene.)

NURSE EATON. When changing the dressing, it is of the utmost importance to wear a sterile glove, keeping your ungloved hand away from the wound. In nurses' training, we learn by tying the excess arm behind our back.

(LIGHTS fade on bench area as FARMER, FARMER'S WIFE and EATON exit with chairs and props.)

NURSE EATON. It's filled with potentially harmful germs. Should the catheter become infected, get to a hospital. I repeat, get to a hospital immediately.

(LIGHTS up on bed area. ELLIS is pacing, wrapped in a voluminous bath towel, eager to begin. Bed is dressed with L.A. quilt.)

ELLIS. It's itchy.
LYNNE. *(Offstage.)* I'm hurrying.
ELLIS. And it's cold.
LYNNE. *(Offstage.)* Almost ready.
ELLIS. This isn't just a dressing change, you know.
LYNNE. *(Offstage.)* I know.
ELLIS. One slip of the clamp and there's an air bubble.

(*LYNNE brings in a chair, covered with dressing kit, opsite bandage, chux, hemostat, and alcohol preps.*)

ELLIS. One slip and the emergency room. That tube leads right to my blood stream, right to my heart. (*Beat.*) Think it's infected?
LYNNE. Don't worry.
ELLIS. "Don't worry." What a dumb thing to say, "Don't worry." Of course, I'm worried. Aren't you worried?
LYNNE. Yes. (*Reads.*) "Wash hands thoroughly." (*Exits narrowly into bathroom, blocking out the* cat.) Move, Holbein.
ELLIS. (*Over SOUND of water.*) My blood count's low! (*Pause for response.*) One germ and it goes right to my blood stream. (*Pause for response.*) She warned us. One germ and I've got infection. (*To herself.*) All I need is infection. (*Beat.*) Is that water hot?
LYNNE. (*Offstage.*) Yes.
ELLIS. Very?
LYNNE. (*Enters narrowly, squeezing out* cat. *Closes door.*) Very.
ELLIS. Wash your hands.
LYNNE. I just washed my hands.
ELLIS. Again.
LYNNE. Why?
ELLIS. You touched the doorknob.

(*LYNNE returns to bathroom, pushing* cat *out of way. SOUND of water.*)

ELLIS. (*Lies down on bed. Vulnerable.*) I'm not sure this bed's such a good idea!
LYNNE. (*Offstage.*) Would you prefer a table?
ELLIS. No. (*Beat.*) You sure that water's hot?
LYNNE. (*Offstage.*) Trust me.

ELLIS. *(To herself.)* Trust her. Terrific. *(Yells.)* This is my life in your hands! *(To herself.)* I hate this. I really do.

(LYNNE enters, squeezing out cat, hands clinically high.)

ELLIS. Be nice to have a mirror.
LYNNE. I just washed my hands.
ELLIS. Never mind.
LYNNE. *(Leans instructions on Ellis' legs. Reads.)* "Place chux beneath shoulder."

(ELLIS glares at Lynne, skeptically.)

LYNNE. While I get you a mirror. *(Exits to bathroom, squeezing out cat.)*
ELLIS. But you just washed your hands.
LYNNE. *(Offstage.)* Something tells me to get you a mirror.

(SOUND of water.)

ELLIS. Something tells me you're stalling.
LYNNE. *(Offstage.)* I'm not stalling.
ELLIS. You're stalling and you're scared. *(Places chux beneath her shoulder.)*
LYNNE. *(Enters with surgically poised hands. Mirror under arm. Narrowly squeezes out the cat.)* Move, Holbein. *(Hips the door shut; passes mirror to Ellis; reads.)* "Remove old dressing carefully." *(An op-site bandage covers the clavicle of Ellis' right shoulder, underneath that a piece of gauze, underneath that a small tube, the heparin tube, dangles auspiciously. LYNNE removes the op-site as if she were defusing an H-bomb. Peeling it off slowly. Hours later:)* That hurt?
ELLIS. It wouldn't if you'd go faster.

(*Finally off, LYNNE looks around for a basket, no basket. SHE tosses bandage on the floor. The small piece of gauze now separates Lynne from the surgical wound. ELLIS watches her intently, as SHE inches off the gauze.*)

ELLIS. What do you see?
LYNNE. A tube going into your shoulder, held down with wings, held down with stitches. And dried blood from the operation.
ELLIS. (*Feigns casual, but her voice betrays her—in the vicinity of* Aida.) Is it red?
LYNNE. No.
ELLIS. Any swelling?
LYNNE. Not that I can see.
ELLIS. What do you mean, not that I can see?
LYNNE. No. No swelling.
ELLIS. All I need is phlebitis.
LYNNE. (*Reads; while cleaning hemostat with alcohol prep.*) "Check sutures to see if they're still tight." (*Pulls squeamishly on sutures.*)
ELLIS. Are they tight?
LYNNE. Yes.
ELLIS. You sure?
LYNNE. (*Not sure at all, but fearful of yanking the sutures out.*) Yes.
ELLIS. You don't sound sure.
LYNNE. "Open dressing kit."

(*Pauses. ELLIS waits impatiently. LYNNE snaps open the kit and drops its plastic wrapping on the floor.*)

ELLIS. Why don't you put it in a basket?
LYNNE. I don't have a basket.

ELLIS. You should have put a basket there.
LYNNE. Too late, now.

(The kit, a clear plastic bucket, is enclosed in butcher's paper, folded like Christmas wrapping. When opened carefully, the butcher's paper becomes the sterile field. SHE tentatively reaches for the first pointed corner.)

ELLIS. Don't touch the inside of it with your fingers, you're going to get germs all over it! The paper's the sterile field!
LYNNE. Okay, okay.
ELLIS. It's going to clot, I know it. All I need is a clot.
LYNNE. *(Pulls each corner of the overwrap to form the sterile field.)* If your eyes get any narrower, you'll look like Charlie Chan. *(Reads.)* "Don first sterile glove. *(Carefully lifts glove out of wrapper.)*
ELLIS. By the inside cuff! If you touch the outside, it won't be sterile. The inside cuff.
LYNNE. Will you settle down! *(Struggles with glove—like an udder gone wild; eroding ELLIS' confidence even more.)* Shit.
ELLIS. It'd be a lot easier without your ring.
LYNNE. *(Trying to maintain her dignity.)* I know that.
ELLIS. Then why's it on?
LYNNE. Because.
ELLIS. Because why?
LYNNE. Because I forgot to take it off, Ollie.

(ELLIS suffers in silence, while LYNNE continues struggling with the glove.)

LYNNE. I'll bet Marcus Welby didn't do this. I'll bet he had a stand-in. Grab the cuff, pull, and snap—who're they kidding? Grab the cuff, pull, and snap—all five fingers in the same damn thumb hole. (*Finally on. With a large bulge.*)

ELLIS. All this and thrombosis.

(*LYNNE puts her ungloved hand behind her back.*)

ELLIS. She suggested you tie your ungloved hand behind your back.

LYNNE. Too late, now.

ELLIS. Isn't it. (*Beat.*) Constantly.

LYNNE. (*Turns toward audience, stares deadpan. Then reads:*) "Place items from container on sterile field, including 4x4's, 2x2's, saving receptacle for pharmaceutical debris." (*Huh? The bucket is filled with pharmaceutical's: gauze, scissors, swab sticks, ointments. LYNNE dumps the contents onto the field and drops the bucket on floor.*)

ELLIS. (*Looks at her through slits:*) You're gonna need that for garbage.

(*LYNNE reaches to pick it up with sterile glove—oops. Instead, picks it up with regular hand and starts to put it on field—oops. ELLIS watches, eyebrow arched, testing. LYNNE drops it back on floor.*)

ELLIS. It's hard not to notice the ineptness of my "Significant Other."

LYNNE. "Use alcohol swabs to clean." I feel like I'm assembling a toy.

ELLIS. Well, you're not.

(*LYNNE picks up packet of swab sticks, selects one, and gingerly cleans around wound.*)

ELLIS. Get it good and clean. (*Pause.*) Scrub harder, I can stand it. First the wings. Then under the wings, under the sutures. Get it all out. (*Beat.*) Clean away from the wound. Concentric circles away from the wound. Never go back inside the circle. Don't contaminate what's already been cleaned. (*Alarmed.*) Did you go back inside?

LYNNE. (*Not sure.*) No.

ELLIS. Why did you say "no"? You're not sure. I can hear it.

LYNNE. Because I fear your temper more than I fear negligent homicide. (*Throws swab stick out; gets another.*)

ELLIS. Clean the whole area.

LYNNE. I am.

ELLIS. (*Uses hand mirror to look.*) Harder.

LYNNE. I am.

ELLIS. I should be doing this myself.

(*LYNNE picks up envelope of solution, concentrating on what SHE can and cannot touch. PHONE rings; BOTH freeze.*)

ELLIS. At least the machine's on. (*Another RING.*) Why isn't the machine on?

LYNNE. I unplugged it while I was painting.

ELLIS. Swell.

(*Guiltily, LYNNE grabs the package by her left, ungloved hand, scissors in right.*)

ELLIS. Could be a job offer.

(*Guiltily, LYNNE cuts the package of solution on a diagonal.*)

ELLIS. What if it's a job offer?

(*Guiltily, LYNNE dips gauze in solution, daubs wound. PHONE stops ringing. There is a slight drip. ELLIS is delighted.*)

ELLIS. It's running.
LYNNE. One drip.
ELLIS. (*Even tone.*) It's getting on the bed.
LYNNE. Will you relax!
ELLIS. I told you this bed was a lousy idea.
LYNNE. Ellis, I swear I'll kill you.
ELLIS. That's obvious.

(*LYNNE leans over Ellis, daubing the pathetic drip with gauze. Her hair lightly touches the site. Tempo accelerates.*)

ELLIS. You got your hair in it!
LYNNE. No, I didn't!
ELLIS. You did! You got your hair in it!
LYNNE. Stop yelling! You're not helping!
ELLIS. It's making a mess! It's running over everything!

(*LYNNE continues to daub.*)

ELLIS. That's enough. That's enough! Don't clean it up with the gauze. You're going outside the sterile field. That's not sterile down there. Did you touch it?
LYNNE. (*Quietly, hoping not to get caught.*) No.
ELLIS. You did, too. Jesus!
LYNNE. Will you stop yelling! You're making me a nervous wreck! The more you yell, the worse I get! You're like a goddam back street surgeon!

(Aware of her faux pas, LYNNE retreats and opens the ointment, hoping ELLIS was deaf. Pace slows. ELLIS is silenced by Lynne's outburst, until ...)

ELLIS. Back street surgeon?
LYNNE. You know what I mean.
ELLIS. You said, "back street."
LYNNE. I meant, "back seat."
ELLIS. You said, "back street."
LYNNE. Damn it! Stop it! *(Metamorphosis. LYNNE becomes the Diabolical Doctor. Pulls off glove, savagely. Pace speeds up as her next syllable sounds like a hiss.)* Discard glove! *(Pulls off first glove, wiggles it; drops it tauntingly on floor.)* Don second glove! *(Dons the second with great prowess. Pulls down on the cuff and lets the glove fly back into place—a la Ben Casey. It is her grand gesture. Proceeds quickly, now—with confidence. Even if the glove has gone on like a cow's udder.)* "Scoop ointment onto site." *(LYNNE does. Drops it onto floor. Reads.)* "Blot dry with sterile gauze. *(Does; throws it defiantly onto floor. Reads.)* "Cover site with 2x2's." *(Places two gauze squares on top.)* "Discard glove." *(Tosses glove maniacally into air.)* "Affix op-site." *(Takes cover off op-site, pulls off backing and slaps it on Ellis. Beat, then:)* Shit.
ELLIS. What?
LYNNE. Shit.
ELLIS. What? What!
LYNNE. The bandage puckered.
ELLIS. Did you touch the sterile site?
LYNNE. Yes.
ELLIS. *(Delighted to be proved right. An idiot has been attending her medically. Oliver Hardy stare.)* Then you'll have to start over, Stanley.

(LYNNE exits.)

ELLIS. *(Mutters.)* I've had enough of this, I really have. Starting Monday, I'm gonna stop being a victim and learn to take care of myself. I'm going to go to gym, go to yoga, and run ten miles around the lake whether I'm tired or not. *(Clamps on headphones; defiantly snaps on Walkman full blast—intro to "Fame": "Baby look at me.")*

(LYNNE returns, sterile hands in air, as ELLIS takes off headphones, SOUND out. ELLIS yells defiantly:)

ELLIS. Starting Monday, I'll be perfect.

(SOUND on as ELLIS clamps on headphones. LIGHTS fade out. HOUSELIGHTS fade up slowly as MUSIC continues.)

End of Act I

ACT II

AT RISE: SOUND: Brandenburg Concerto.
FADEUP. A cozy portrait. HELEN is sitting on the bench, wrapping a Christmas present. LYNNE is stretched out on floor reading an Isocal pamphlet while stirring a bucket of yellow paint.

LYNNE. (*Reads.*) "Weight loss occurs because the disease and its treatments decrease appetite. Dry mouth decreases appetite; nausea decreases appetite; decreased appetite decreases appetite." Swell. (*Suddenly, there is a piercing* cri de coeur *from the kitchen.*)
ELLIS. (*Offstage.*) I can't stand it any longer!

(*LYNNE looks up—startled. HELEN continues wrapping.*)

ELLIS. (*Offstage.*) I don't know where anything is! There are pans in the plates, plates in the pans, forks in the knives, and every cupboard door is open! (*Bang.*) Were we born in a barn!
LYNNE. (*Waits. "Cri" over? Back to pamphlet. Then to Helen.*) Oh, you're gonna love this. Things we can make: Isocal Eggnog, Isocal Banana Blush ...
ELLIS. (*Offstage.*) I can't stand it any longer! Everything in this refrigerator is moldy. The rice, the beans, the moo shu pork. And where's the jelly lid? Look at this! Look at this!
LYNNE. (*To Helen.*) Look at what?
ELLIS. (*Offstage.*) Look at this refrigerator! Little dabs of left over everything. No wonder we can't find the egglplant. Mr. Keene *and all his lost persons* couldn't find

61

the eggplant. I found the jelly lid! (*The news has little impact.*) Even the jelly lid's moldy. And what's in the tin foil?

LYNNE. (*Under her breath to Helen.*) Last week's pizza?

HELEN. Could be that, could be fish.

ELLIS. (*Offstage.*) Tomorrow morning at 9 a.m. there will be an autopsy on this pizza.

(*HELEN stands up.*)

LYNNE. I think she needs you.

HELEN. Uh, uh. Not in that mood. I learned a long time ago to leave her alone. (*Exits with wrappings.*)

(*Silence, only the sound of the* Brandenburg Concerto. *LYNNE returns to pamphlet. Then: ROAR of an engine from offstage. ELLIS careens around the corner pushing the front part or hose of a vacuum cleaner, sans canister. LYNNE turns the pages of the pamphlet.*)

ELLIS. (*Yells above the roar:*) The sea salt does not belong in the medicine cabinet.

(*LYNNE lifts feet on cue.*)

ELLIS. The toothpaste, however, does.

(*LYNNE stares deadpan at audience.*)

ELLIS. Every cup, saucer, and plate we own is in the dishwasher. Are we packing it to move? (*ELLIS switches off vacuum.*) Wonderful, now she's stirring paint in the living room. Are you stirring paint in the living room?

(*LYNNE nods her head "yes."*)

ELLIS. Are you getting it on the floor?

(*LYNNE shakes her head "no."*)

ELLIS. I'll bet you're getting it on the floor. Tell me that's not yellow. Is that yellow?

(*LYNNE nods her head "yes."*)

ELLIS. The whole kitchen's yellow. The walls are yellow; the cupboards are yellow. Even the pepper mill's yellow. Why is the pepper mill yellow?
LYNNE. I had some paint left.
ELLIS. Well, I hope you ran out of stencilled roosters. (*Switches on VACUUM, looks away from Lynne.*)

(*LYNNE looks at audience, shakes her heard "no."*)

ELLIS. (*Switches off vacuum.*) I saw that!
LYNNE. You said you liked "country"!
ELLIS. That's not "country."
LYNNE. Then what is it?
ELLIS. Enchanted cottage.
LYNNE. You want it painted, or you want it perfect?
ELLIS. Aren't we late for my heparin shot?
LYNNE. Ooh, right. Just give me time to find a marker.
ELLIS. Time. Take your time. I've got all the time in the world.
LYNNE. (*Rips page out of pamphlet.*) I found a marker.
ELLIS. I knew it was going to come to this.
LYNNE. Ellis, I'm here to help. Tell me how to help.

ELLIS. You can help by being less controlling.

LYNNE. (*Leaps up a la Rumplestilskin.*) I'm controlling! I'm controlling!

ELLIS. (*Winds vacuum cord with pseudo-nonchalance, inwardly frightened by the intensity of Lynne's anger.*) Yes.

LYNNE. Are you crazy! How, in God's name, am I the one that's controlling?

ELLIS. Demanding I be rational is controlling. (*Exits to bed area.*)

LYNNE. (*Furious. A little Gleason:*) Bang, pow, zoom! (*Pauses. Then to audience.*) You know, she's right.

(*HELEN enters with tray containing: mug, heparin needle inserted into tubex, alcohol prep, and assorted socks. LYNNE gives bucket to Helen, drapes socks over her shoulder, takes tray while addressing audience. HELEN exits.*)

LYNNE. I kept thinking about this kid I saw at a garden party—running 'round and 'round in a circle. 'Round the tables, 'round the buffet. Faster and faster. You could see she was exhausted but she'd just go faster. Then she began to scream: "Stop me! Stop me! Somebody, please, stop me!"

(*CROSS FADE. ELLIS is under L.A. quilt; nose deep in book. LYNNE enters with tray.*)

LYNNE. (*Hesitant.*) I brought you some soup. (*No response.*) It's your favorite: cream of mushroom. (*No response.*) Sixty calories. Eighty, if you use whole milk. We used whole milk. (*Sets tray on bed table.*)

ELLIS. Why do I do that? (*Beat.*) Why do I do it?

LYNNE. (*A Viennese psychiatrist.*) Tell me about your mother.

ELLIS. Speaking of whom?

LYNNE. (*Opens alcohol prep.*) In the refrigerator. Looking for the eggplant.

ELLIS. She doesn't have to.

LYNNE. Try and tell her that.

ELLIS. (*Unbuttons top of shirt or blouse; holds heparin cap toward Lynne.*) I told you you wouldn't like me when you saw all of me.

LYNNE. (*Cleans heparin cap with alcohol pad.*) I saw all of you when we met. Slowly but surely, I'm seeing less and less.

ELLIS. Have you noticed these books say the same thing. "Let go of the oars." "Flow with the river." "Let it pass, let it be, let go." I keep thinking, that's so trite, that's so corny. They all say the same thing: Psychiatry, religion, A.A., Jesus Christ ...

LYNNE. (*Expertly releases air bubble from needle.*) Paul McCartney.

ELLIS. I don't need a relationship; I need a nanny. Why do you put up with it?

LYNNE. (*In her best Mouseketeer.*) "Why? Because we love you."

ELLIS. That's what I mean—why?

LYNNE. (*Gives Ellis heparin shot.*) Your vulnerability.

ELLIS. I thought the world liked tough.

LYNNE. Vulnerability. And you've sure got a lot to love. Eat your soup.

(*ELLIS starts to eat.*)

LYNNE. Jesus God, it's cold in this house. (*Crawls under covers at foot of bed, folds socks.*)

(*ELLIS stops eating.*)

LYNNE. What's wrong?
ELLIS. (*Staring into soup.*) I'm not very hungry.
LYNNE. But you love cream of mushroom.
ELLIS. (*Hesitation; not wanting to hurt.*) It has lumps in it.
LYNNE. It always has lumps.
ELLIS. Not when Mom fixes it. I got a job offer today. (*Sets mug on tray.*) Primetime television. Not an interview—a definite job offer.
LYNNE. When does it start?
ELLIS. Two months. (*Silence.*) Well, we don't know if I'll be dead. Where should I have my ashes scattered? (*Beat.*) How 'bout Island Beach? How 'bout the inlet at Barnegat Bay? (*Beat.*) I can't hear out of my left ear.
LYNNE. (*Feels Ellis' shoulder.*) Since when?
ELLIS. Since yesterday.
LYNNE. Why didn't you tell me yesterday?
ELLIS. I wasn't frightened yesterday.
ELLIS. (*Laughs.*) What are the signs of a brain tumor? (*Softly.*) Help me.
LYNNE. How?
ELLIS. Push the fear away.
LYNNE. Let it in.
ELLIS. Oh, please. That's not what I need.
LYNNE. That is what you need. It is, Ellis. (*Entreats.*) Don't turn away, listen to me. Will you listen? You're like a soldier defending a bunker, piling up layer after layer of sandbags to protect yourself from pain. And you know what the joke is? You're only sealing it in. What's down there that's so frightening? What's down there that's so bad?
ELLIS. A barn filled with slime.

LYNNE. Then clean it out. Why would you want to live in it? Clean it out.

ELLIS. I want to die unafraid. With dignity, unafraid.

LYNNE. First you have to live unafraid. I know "look who's talking." (*Laughs.*) We're quite a pair. I'm afraid to go outside; you're afraid to go inside.

HELEN. (*Hurries onstage.*) I found the eggplant! (*Looks at watch.*) My God, it's 2 a.m. (*Exits.*)

ELLIS. There's a two-week intensive in Ojai ["o-hi"] Lot of meditating. (*Silence.*) Lot of people.

LYNNE. (*Shudders; long silence.*) Look, I'll make a deal with you. I'll face the people; you face yourself.

ELLIS. You're asking me to dig out thirty-eight years of shit.

LYNNE. I'll grab a shovel, we'll work fast.

(*BOTH laugh; ELLIS coughs; takes Lynne's finger; studies it.*)

LYNNE. From making cole slaw. I grated my finger.

(*ELLIS looks at Lynne's thumb.*)

LYNNE. Razor cut. From scraping beautiful Victorian windows. (*Looks at palms of hands.*) Grass stains. Pulling vines. (*LYNNE shows Ellis hairless arms.*) Singed. Everytime I light the oven. (*Show another spot on fingers.*) Pinched. From setting up your mother's bed. (*Reparts hair.*) This is where Johnny Danielson hit me with a bat. (*Shows top of foot.*) This is where Lois Eby [Ee-bee] stabbed me with a lead pencil.

ELLIS. You remember every scar?

LYNNE. Every scar.

ELLIS. Even the ones I give you?

LYNNE. Every scar.

ELLIS. Don't pay me back, okay?

(*CROSS-FADE. ELLIS crosses to neutral area; LYNNE puts tray and socks under bed, then crosses DS to audience.*)

LYNNE. Picasso once said: a friend is someone you can sleep with. He wasn't talking about sex; he was talking about touch. There's a physical honesty as well as a mental honesty. I think it was Picasso.

(*LIGHTS on ELLIS, eyes closed, meditating in lotus position.*)

LYNNE. I thought it was Picasso. (*Sits next to Ellis, shifts into lotus.*) I'd like it to be Picasso. (*SOUND: George Winston; to Ellis.*) I want you to know we look ridiculous.

ELLIS. Concentrate on the mantra; exclude all thoughts.

LYNNE. Easy for you. (*To audience.*) Would someone please explain this to my mother. I come from a sensible state. Michigan. You don't do this in Michigan. And if you do, you lock the door. (*Beat.*) I lost all sense of dignity. The first day we sat around in high lotus doing "Introductions." I hate: "Introductions." I sit there rehearsing my name. Then we had to conjure up a power animal to be our guide. The first guy saw a tiger. My turn: I saw nothing. The next saw an eagle; the next a hawk. My turn: I saw nothing. They told me to let my mind drift, meander through the woods. And there, at the edge of a glen, I saw my power animal. I had to tell them it looked a lot like Thumper. (*Closes eyes, meditates.*)

ELLIS. (*Opens eyes, to herself.*) Ardis says temper tantrums are my speciality. I learned their power early. I think Mom found it easier to give in than live through one. When I was upset I'd go to my room and sulk, hoping she'd follow. She never did. I guess she just wanted to give me privacy. I thought she didn't care. Maybe that's why I care about Lynne. She doesn't stay outside the door. But sometimes I punish her for it. I don't know why. *(Closes eyes.)*

LYNNE. *(Opens eyes; to audience.)* I've always been terrified of hippies; I think they know something I don't. Truth be told, my other great terror was Ingmar Bergman movies. I was so relieved when I found out they weren't over my head. *(Beat.)* Can a person with average intelligence flunk meditating? I mean, maybe I don't have a higher consciousness; maybe my brain stops at the mezzanine. Thank you for sharing. *(Closes eyes; meditates.)*

ELLIS. *(Opens eyes; to herself.)* For so long I wanted out. But I don't think that's true anymore. I have to admit, the house looks nice. When I'm not being perfect. When I'm not being a perfect shit. *(Beat.)* I love my dog. I love my cat. *(Looks at Lynne; looks away.)* I'd very much like to live. *(Closes eyes.)*

LYNNE. *(To audience.)* One night I dreamt that Ellis died alone. That was my biggest fear. It's such an intimate thing, death. Why in hospitals, why with strangers? *(Motions toward Ellis.)* Look at her. I mean, that's serious meditating. I'll bet she's on the 17th floor.

ELLIS. *(To Lynne.)* Bargain basement, smart ass. *(Looks at watch; stands up.)* Three o'clock. Dance time.

LYNNE. I hate it.

ELLIS. I love it.

LYNNE. Sure. You look good in a leotard.

ELLIS. Then don't do it. Speak up.

LYNNE. (*Stands up.*) Speak up, she says. Speaking up makes you visible. You want to walk around visible? I sure don't.

ELLIS. I thought we had a deal.

LYNNE. I'll speak up.

(*LIGHTING change. LYNNE exits. BENBERG enters studying a chart; TRISH carries a clipboard.*)

TRISH. How you feeling?

ELLIS. Four months done; none to go. Shouldn't I be dead?

BENBERG. (*Feels her shoulder.*) If you come here five years from now and call me an ass, I won't be surprised. Cancer's unpredictable.

ELLIS. I can't hear out of my left ear.

BENBERG. Pain?

ELLIS. Terror. (*Laughs; coughs.*) What are the signs of a brain tumor?

BENBERG. I think we should try something else.

ELLIS. What's left?

BENBERG. A Chinese plant.

(*ELLIS looks at him.*)

BENBERG. Would I kid you?

(*TRISH hands Ellis paper to sign.*)

BENBERG. You'd be guinea pig Number 3. And you'd have to stay in Houston, as an in-patient.

ELLIS. (*Looks at paper.*) Homoharringtonine?

TRISH. Great stuff.

(*Escorts Ellis across stage to bed area as BENBERG exits. Swirl of activity as ELLIS goes offstage and changes into hospital gown. TRISH changes the bed to hospital white. NURSE brings in IV pole and places it US of bed. MALE NURSE brings in a blanketed cot SR (Ellis' robe on top) and sets it between Ellis' bed and window, paralleling the bed. NURSE and MALE NURSE exit.*)

TRISH. Where's Lynne?
ELLIS. (*Offstage.*) Getting me toothpaste. (*Enters.*) See these are the biggies, do you get travel size or economy size when you're told you have three months to live? (*Coughs.*)

(*TRISH tucks ELLIS in bed; inserts IV line into Ellis' arm; takes remote off bed table and turns on flying TV. SOUND: Academy Awards bump loudly on: APPLAUSE, MUSIC, the reading of the nominees. TRISH uses remote to lower the sound. ELLIS gets out journal.*)

LYNNE. (*Enters SL with grocery bag; to audience.*) It was April, 1983. I remember because it was Academy Award night. Better known as "The Night They Ignored E.T." Best Film Editing: *Ghandi*. Best Screen play: *Ghandi* Best Location Caterer: *Ghandi*.
ELLIS. (*From hospital bed.*) At least they didn't get "Best Cancer Patient." I got best cancer patient.

(*TRISH sits at foot of bed, glances up at TV. ELLIS writes in journal, thinks, erases. LYNNE crosses to bed area. SHE is a whirlwind of movement: sets grocery bag on bed table; refolds Ellis' robe, sets it on side of bed.*)

LYNNE. They put patients' first names outside each door. Your "S" fell off. You're now "Elli Crowley." (*Looks at IV.*) Who's that?

TRISH. He just won for best short animated ... and won't get off the stage.

(*ELLIS writes; erases.*)

TRISH. What're you doing?

ELLIS. Ardis says to list all the ways to punish people without punishing myself.

LYNNE. She's been at that for two days.

ELLIS. Even my moderation is excessive.

BLOOD NURSE. (*Enters with blood caddy. Talks to Ellis loudly, as if she's deaf. Talks softly to others.*) I have to get some blood, Mrs. Crowley.

ELLIS. Miss. It's Miss Crowley.

LYNNE. They just did that this morning.

BLOOD NURSE. It won't hurt.

ELLIS. Yes, it will. (*To Blood Nurse.*) I hope you're the best. I don't have any veins left.

BLOOD NURSE. Only take a minute.

(*LYNNE watches, helplessly, while BLOOD NURSE swabs Ellis' arm, stabs and ELLIS winces; mumbles into bag.*)

LYNNE. They just did that this morning. (*Takes out groceries; holds each on high before setting on bed table.*) Papaya Sunrise, Two hundred-fifty calories ... Toothpaste. (*Takes an enormous tube of toothpaste out of bag.*)

ELLIS. (*Coughs.*) That's a little optimistic, don't you think?

LYNNE. Haagen-Daz vanilla fudge ... (*Takes off lid.*) Twenty glorious calories every glorious spoonful. (*Inserts spoon.*) Eat. (*Sets ice cream on bed table.*)

ELLIS. (*Continues to write; erase.*) I ate.

LYNNE. You tossed. Eat. You've only had six hundred-fifty calories so far today. (*Takes toothpaste into bathroom.*)

ELLIS. It burns.

LYNNE. (*Offstage.*) Ice cream burns?

TRISH. It's the medicine.

LYNNE. (*Comes out of bathroom; to Trish.*) Her mouth's so dry it burns?

ELLIS. (*Writes in journal, erases.*) Will you slow down? Sit. Watch the show. (*Points to IV.*)

(*LYNNE sits, watches BLOOD NURSE withdraw needle and stab again.*)

LYNNE. (*Mutters.*) They just did that this morning. (*Looks away.*)

TRISH. (*Tries to divert Ellis' attention from needle.*) How much television did you direct?

ELLIS. None of them count.

LYNNE. Plenty count. What about the soap? Doesn't a year on a soap count?

ELLIS. How can it? I got fired.

LYNNE. (*For the last time.*) You *weren't* fired. (*To Trish.*) Why the hell she'd choose directing, I'll never know. Out of sixty thousand hours of primetime television only one hundred-thirty-five were directed by women.

ELLIS. Thirty-five of those by Ida Lupino. (*ELLIS winces; wince turns to cough.*)

BLOOD NURSE. You got a cough, too? I had a cough all day yesterday. Took NyQuil and slept like a baby. Just took NyQuil. (*Withdraws needle; stabs again.*) Your vein keeps rolling.

    LYNNE. (*Looking at* IV.) Oh oh.

    ELLIS. What?

    LYNNE. They've been raiding the motion picture home again.

    TRISH. (*Looking at* IV.) My God, is he still alive?

    LYNNE. He'll never make it to the podium.

    TRISH. Is he still alive?

    LYNNE. Why do they wait to honor them in their nineties?

    ELLIS. They prefer near death. Or just after. You're no longer a threat.

    LYNNE. He'll never make it to the podium.

    BENBERG. (*Enters.*) Evening, ladies.

    TRISH. You still here?

    BENBERG. I'm still here; you still here? (*Glances at* IV.) My God, is he still here?

(*ALL watch. MALE NURSE wanders on, watches. Long pause.*)

    LYNNE. He made it! (*Cheers.*)

    ELLIS. I hate to throw a damper on all this enthusiasm, but he still has to open the envelope.

(*Overlapping mutters.*)

    MALE NURSE. Well, guess I'll go finish my coffee.

    BENBERG. Are there any donuts left?

    TRISH. Donuts? Did someone say "donuts?"

    BLOOD NURSE. (*Withdraws needle; to Trish.*) Her veins keep rolling.

    TRISH. (*Stops at door; softly.*) Who's the best? Are you the best?

BLOOD NURSE. Christine's the best.

(*TRISH continues to look at her.*)

BLOOD NURSE. I'll get Christine. (*Exits.*)
TRISH. (*To Lynne.*) It's cold by that window. I'll find you more blankets. (*Exits.*)
ELLIS. (*Writes, erases.*) Damn.
LYNNE. What?
ELLIS. There aren't any ways to punish people without punishing myself.
LYNNE. I wondered how long it'd take you to figure that out.
ELLIS. Did you pay her?
LYNNE. (*Turns off TV with remote control on bed table; to audience.*) We finally settled down for sleep. (*Sits on cot; covers herself.*) But the night was far from over. (*Reaches up to switch; turns light off.*)

(*BLACKOUT. FADE-UP faint LIGHT: the MOON the only source. LYNNE is between the bed and the window, sleeping on the cot. SHE pulls sheet blanket around her ears, freezing. ELLIS sits up in bed, looks around, climbs out, and walks to the window. The IV pole, however, remains by her bed. As the tubes are still attached to her body, the lines become taut with each step. They wake LYNNE with a start as they snake across her bed. SHE sees the pole tipping precariously and bolts up.*)

LYNNE. What are you doing!
ELLIS. (*Looks at Lynne; puzzled by the alarm, then calmly.*) Looking out the window.
LYNNE. But the pole!
ELLIS. (*Calmly.*) What?

LYNNE. The pole! Don't move!
ELLIS. (*Calmly.*) Why are you yelling?
LYNNE. Don't move! (*Leaps out of bed; switches on LIGHT; grabs pole.*) You're going to pull the catheter right out of your arm. Trust me, don't move.

(*Walks ELLIS toward the bed.*)

LYNNE. God, you scared me. Geezus, it's 5 AM.
ELLIS. (*Like a child, an amnesiac.*) I'm sorry.
LYNNE. It wasn't your fault. You're still asleep. (*Helps her into bed.*) I've never seen you like that.
ELLIS. Like what?
LYNNE. Like that. So out of it.
ELLIS. Why are you sleeping?
LYNNE. Pardon me?
ELLIS. (*Points at pole.*) Why are you sleeping? (*Her voice even, low—emotionless. Almost robotic.*)
LYNNE. Are you trying to say "pole"?
ELLIS. Yes.
LYNNE. Honey, you're not making any sense.
ELLIS. You're not either.
LYNNE. But you're pointing at the pole.
ELLIS. Yes. (*Begins picking at her hospital gown.*)
LYNNE. (*Long pause.*) Ellis, what's wrong?
ELLIS. Nothing.
LYNNE. Do you know where you are?
ELLIS. In a hospital?
LYNNE. You're not sure?
ELLIS. It looks like a hospital.
LYNNE. It is a hospital.
ELLIS. (*Her questions are soft, sweet.*) Am I sick?
LYNNE. You don't know?
ELLIS. I guess I am.
LYNNE. Ellis ... you have cancer.

ELLIS. (*Emotionless.*) Oh.
LYNNE. You don't remember?
ELLIS. No.
LYNNE. Not anything?
ELLIS. No. (*Picks at her gown.*)
LYNNE. What year is this?
ELLIS. 1978.
LYNNE. Where do you live?
ELLIS. West 87th.
LYNNE. New York?
ELLIS. Yes.
LYNNE. (*A little too harshly; alarmed.*) You live in L.A.

(*ELLIS, puzzled silence; chastised.*)

LYNNE. (*Terrified, but gentler.*) Don't be scared.
ELLIS. (*Her voice remains emotionless.*) I'm not scared.
LYNNE. Ellis, think. Please. What year is this?
ELLIS. 1967.
LYNNE. Where do you live?
ELLIS. East 14th.
LYNNE. I'll be right back. Stay in bed; I'll be right back.

(*Runs off. Hurries back, trailed by NURSE EATON and MALE NURSE. HE scans his clipboard.*)

NURSE EATON. (*As if addressing a four-year-old.*) Hello, Elli.
ELLIS. (*Like said four-year-old.*) Hello.
LYNNE. (*Overlap; softly.*) Ellis. It's Ellis.
NURSE EATON. How are you feeling?
ELLIS. Okay.

NURSE EATON. Do you know where you are?
ELLIS. A hospital.
NURSE EATON. Do you know why?
ELLIS. (*Sweetly.*) Yes.
NURSE EATON. Why?
ELLIS. I have cancer.
NURSE EATON. (*Looks at Lynne with "she's fine."*) What year is this?
ELLIS. 1953.
NURSE EATON. Where do you live?
ELLIS. Westbury Avenue.

(*NURSE EATON looks to Lynne for verification; as does ELLIS.*)

LYNNE. Long Island?
ELLIS. Yes. (*Wanting to please.*) Is that wrong?
LYNNE. When she was nine. (*Off-hand.*) Is it in the brain?
NURSE EATON. (*To Male Nurse.*) Call Chawla.

(*BOTH exit. LYNNE sits on side of bed. ELLIS watches her closely, like a child who has done something wrong. THEY have nothing to say to each other. NURSE EATON returns with* pill *and paper cup.*)

LYNNE. What's that?
NURSE EATON. Benadryl. (*Hands pill to Ellis.*)
LYNNE. Isn't it possible—with all these drugs she's getting—isn't it possible they backed up on her? That she overdosed?
NURSE EATON. Possible.
LYNNE. If the liver can't detox poisons, it can't detox drugs either. Isn't it possible?
NURSE EATON. Possible.

LYNNE. Can't you wait; can't we find out?
NURSE EATON. (*Hands paper cup to Ellis.*) The doctor prescribed it.
LYNNE. When? Just now? Is it in the brain? (*Watches helplessly.*)

(*ELLIS takes pill as MALE NURSE and NURSE enter.*)

NURSE EATON. (*Begins a rote exchange preoccupied with IV bottle.*) How are you Eli? Do you know where you are?
MALE NURSE. What year is it? What month? Do you know where you are?

(*Litany continues softly, overlapping LYNNE and eventually TRISH:*)

NURSE EATON. What year is it? What month?
MALE NURSE. Do you know where you are?
NURSE. What year is it? What month? Do you know where you are?

(*LYNNE paces apron as muted litany continues. LIGHTING changes to early morning. TRISH enters wearing a coat; crosses directly to Lynne.*)

TRISH. Do you have power of attorney? Anything signed?

(*LYNNE shakes head "no."*)

TRISH. You're not related, that's trouble. If they put her on life supports, you can't get her off. She needs your protection and right now you can't protect her. Where's her mother?

LYNNE. On a plane, Newark to L.A. Or picking up the animals. I tried to leave her a message at the house, but the machine's not picking up. Is it in the brain?

TRISH. (*Puts hand on Lynne's shoulder.*) They don't know.

LYNNE. Oh God, don't be kind. I'll never make it if you're kind.

TRISH. (*Hurries to join questioners.*) Ellis, it's Trish.

MALE NURSE. What year is it? What month?

NURSE EATON. Do you know where you are?

ELLIS. In a hospital.

NURSE EATON. Why?

ELLIS. I'm sick.

NURSE EATON. With what?

ELLIS. Cancer.

MALE NURSE. What year is it?

ELLIS. 1983.

(*LYNNE stands; attentive.*)

TRISH. What month?

ELLIS. April.

TRISH. Where do you live?

ELLIS. Los Angeles.

TRISH. (*Points to Lynne.*) Who is this?

ELLIS. Lynne.

NURSE EATON. Is she your sister?

ELLIS. No. (*Beat.*) She's my friend.

(*TRISH helps ELLIS off. NURSE changes bed to L.A. quilt. MALE NURSE adds clothes to bed, puts pillow on floor, presetting robbery scene, then exits carrying empty IV bottle.*)

LYNNE. (*Walks out of scene. To audience.*) I was never so glad to see anyone in my life. It *was* an overdose. And I was so glad, I cried. I was so glad, I more than cried. I was so glad, I had a teensy nervous breakdown in the corner. Ellis saw it. Ellis shouldn't have seen it. Ellis shouldn't have seen this, either.

(*SOUND: Airport traffic—ground and air. LIGHTS CROSS-FADE from bed area to apron. LYNNE hurries across stage.*)

SKYCAP (*Offstage.*) You can't park there, lady!
LYNNE. (*Yells to Skycap, SL.*) I'm not parking, I'm just loading ...
SKYCAP. (*Offstage.*) You can't park there!
LYNNE. But my friend's sick, I have to ...
SKYCAP. (*Offstage.*) Okay, two minutes.
LYNNE. Right. Two minutes. (*Hurries off.*)

(*LOS ANGELES COP enters; wearing motorcycle helmet; saunters to car; looks at plates; takes out book, starts to write parking ticket. LYNNE enters pushing ELLIS in a wheelchair; yells to him, confident of explanation.*)

LYNNE. He said, "Two minutes." He said I could park there for two minutes.
L.A. COP. You lose, ma'am. (*Shrugs; keeps writing.*)
LYNNE. (*Leaves Ellis SR; runs over to L.A. Cop to confide.*) Look, she's sick, we've got a mound of luggage, I've gotta race to the carousel, race back ... give me a break.
L.A. COP. (*Keeps writing.*) I already wrote out the ticket.
LYNNE. Then unwrite it.
L.A. COP. I can't unwrite it

LYNNE. Then I'll unwrite it!

L.A. COP. (*Calmly.*) Go right ahead, ma'am, and you'll cool off in jail. (*Hand her ticket.*)

LYNNE. But he said, "Two minutes."

(*HE moves to next car; turning his back on her. Long pause. ELLIS watches as LYNNE explodes.*)

LYNNE. Don't you dare turn away from me. Don't you dare! I'm talking to you, Charlie!

(*HE looks at plates of next car; writing up another ticket.*)

LYNNE. That's right shrug your shoulders! Turn away and shrug your shoulders! You lose, ma'am? Just like that, you lose? Big guy with a badge, writing parking tickets. Big guy with a badge! You must be some brave hero to your kids, you sadistic son of a ...!

L.A. COP. (*Turns; nose to nose.*) Don't push me, lady! I swear I'll haul you in. Don't push me! Now get in that car and get out of here!

(*THEY glare at each other; HE turns, walks off. As HE disappears offstage, LYNNE watches his back, ELLIS watches Lynn. Then LYNNE screams.*)

LYNNE. "Two minutes!" HE SAID, "TWO MINUTES!"

(*LYNNE pushes ELLIS in wheelchair as LIGHTS CROSS-FADE to bed area. The bed is mussed, pillow is on floor.*)

HELEN. (*Enters.*) They got the lamps. The police said make a list. They got the lamps; they got the TV. They got your jewelry; they got the answering machine. They got the washer; they got the dryer ...

LYNNE. (*Looks at the devastation.*) They get the checkbooks?

HELEN. They got the checkbooks; they got the stereo.

LYNNE. Should we go to a hotel?

(*ELLIS shakes her head "no."*)

LYNNE. But you can't sleep here, this room's a mess. (*Cleans off bed; three or four pieces of clothing fall to the floor.*)

HELEN. Want some soup? Cereal?

(*ELLIS shakes her head "no."*)

HELEN. Cinnamon toast, lots of butter?

(*ELLIS coughs.*)

HELEN. I'll make some toast. (*Exiting.*) They got the scale; they got the typewriter. They got the clock; they got the other clock.

(*ELLIS gets out of wheelchair.*)

LYNNE. (*Rushes to help.*) Careful, there's glass. (*Helps her slowly into bed.*) How many you think there were? Two, three? (*Taking off Ellis' shoes.*) I'll clean this up right away. At least the clothes. I'll wash the clothes. No I won't. (*Mimics Helen.*) They got the washer, they got the dryer. (*Exits with wheelchair.*)

HELEN. (*Offstage.*) They got the juicer; they got the can opener. (*Head around corner.*) They got the toaster. No toast. (*Beat.*) Want a malt? Nevermind, they got the blender. How 'bout ...

(*ELLIS shakes her head "no."*)

HELEN. (*Feels chastised.*) Look at Holbein. She loves to sleep on that chair. Ever since Lynne got that cover, she stopped sleeping on the couch.

LYNNE. (*Enters.*) She's no fool; it's got cat hair.

HELEN. (*Exiting.*) They got the Polaroid; they got the photos ...

ELLIS. (*Coughs, a deep wrenching cough.*) May I have some water?

LYNNE. Sure. (*Exits to bathroom; SOUND of water. Offstage.*) The good news is: they cleaned out the medicine cabinet. The bad news is: they left the Water-Pic. (*Enters; hands cup to Ellis; sits on bed.*)

(*ELLIS coughs. Silence, then:*)

LYNNE. (*With difficulty.*) Trish thinks we should talk about contingencies.

ELLIS. What contingencies.

LYNNE. I should know your wishes, get Power of Attorney.

ELLIS. Why now?

LYNNE. It can wait 'til tomorrow.

ELLIS. But why now?

LYNNE. I guess she's just thinking ahead.

ELLIS. Way ahead, don't you think.

LYNNE. I didn't ...

ELLIS. You sure didn't. (*Beat.*) Does it mean you'd have power over me?

LYNNE. I could run off with the funds.

ELLIS. You could, you know.

LYNNE. Jesus. (*Long pause.*) Better get some sleep. I'll tiptoe when I come in.

ELLIS. Do you have to?

LYNNE. Come in? (*Yes.*) Course not. (*Stands up; takes cup from Ellis.*) Don't be alone, if you don't have to, okay? (*Beat.*) Well. Need a pillow. (*Picks pillow up.*) Wonderful, they took the pillow case. (*Kneels on floor; looks under bed.*) I just saw one. Hang on, I'm out of here. (*Rummages further; faster.*) Hell with it. I'll use a sweatshirt. (*Rummaging.*) Now where's a sweatshirt? (*Beat.*) Forget the sweatshirt, I'm out of here. (*Waits; wants more; gets nothing. Exits.*)

HELEN. (*A beat, then HELEN enters.*) They got the card table; they got the chairs (*Sits on bed; looks at Holbein.*) Look at Holbein. Animals are so peaceful

ELLIS. Of course, they are. They don't know they're gonna die.

HELEN. (*Chides with humor.*) What a thing to say.

(*ELLIS grabs onto Helen.*)

HELEN. It'll be okay. (*Holds her.*) It'll be okay. (*Continues to hold her.*) Don't worry. It'll be okay. (*Jumps up; reverts to cheerleader.*) I've got it! Root beer float! You used to love root beer floats! I'll fix you a root beer float! (*HELEN exits.*)

(*CROSS-FADE to LYNNE, neutral area.*)

LYNNE. (*Holding bowl of soup; to audience.*) Ellis went so far inward, we couldn't find her. It was like *Invasion of the Body Snatchers*. Remember that movie? All the townspeople are zombies, except for Kevin McCarthy and Dana Wynter, who are in love and trying to escape. He keeps begging her, "Stay awake, don't fall asleep! Stay awake!" Then he leaves her in a cave and she nods off; when he returns, she looks at him with lifeless eyes. Same face, same mannerisms, but lifeless eyes. No love in them. (*Beat.*) That was the most horrifying moment in any horror movie I ever saw. (*Delivers bowl to Ellis.*) There aren't any lumps. We strained it with cheese cloth. (*Waits for response; no response; to audience.*) We were the butt end of a cosmic joke: When she pulled away, I grabbed on. And the more I clutched, the more she pulled away. It was a wonderful cycle. And did I get good.

(*HELEN enters, sets blankets for next scene at foot of bed, takes bowl from Ellis, exits.*)

LYNNE. Boy, did we get good. For five days, we cooked, we sewed, we cooked, we painted. The more she withdrew, the gooder we got. (*Kneels on bedroom floor; to audience.*) I bought her a VCR. (*Adjusts.*) Took me ten years to hook it up. (*To Ellis.*) *Ragtime* or *Midnight Express*?

ELLIS. Either.

LYNNE. *Midnight Express.* (*Turns it on. SOUND of movie.*) Hey, it works! (*Looks to Ellis for applause.*)

(*ELLIS stares at set in silence.*)

LYNNE. (*To audience.*) The illness became our universe. I was three months behind on the Falkland Islands. I had no idea who won. But I had learned one thing: cancer eats up two thousand calories a day. All by itself.

(*HELEN enters, sweeps floor with a broom.*
LYNNE turns to ELLIS who is writing in journal.)

LYNNE. There's a two-week intensive next week in the desert. They said they'd make room for two more.
ELLIS. Can we afford it?
LYNNE. I've got credit cards.
ELLIS. Aren't they at their limit?
LYNNE. I'll get new ones; I'll borrow from friends.
ELLIS. What if I get worse?
LYNNE. I'll bring you home.
ELLIS. Who's going to monitor my blood?
LYNNE. They said there's a doctor, he can take your blood. Then I'll take it to a hospital in Barstow.
ELLIS. Next time you make plans, want to include me?
LYNNE. Sorry. (*Dares.*) But why don't you sleep on it. (*Silence; jokes.*) Stay out of your personal sphere? (*Silence.*) Ellis, talk to me.
ELLIS. (*Furious.*) Stop telling me what to do!

(*HELEN starts to tiptoe off with broom.*)

LYNNE. (*Backs off, quickly.*) Sorry. I'm really sorry.
ELLIS. (*To Lynne.*) And stop tiptoeing!

(*HELEN stops tiptoeing abruptly; exits.*)

LYNNE. I said I was sorry.
ELLIS. You make me feel like a monster! Always tiptoeing!

(*LYNNE is silent.*)

ELLIS. Swell, now she's gonna pout. You gonna pout? You're acting just like my mother. (*Beat.*) I can't do this. I really can't. We met speaking a different language. We're still speaking a different language. I really can't take this turmoil. I need time alone.

LYNNE. I've left you alone.

ELLIS. I need time alone.

LYNNE. Are you saying tonight? (*Silence.*) Are you saying tomorrow? (*Silence.*) What are you saying? (*Silence.*) Small word. Three letters. Sounds like ...

ELLIS. Sometimes I don't think I love you as much as you love me.

LYNNE. Jesus, where'd that come from? (*It landed.*) I'll make a deal with you. I won't ask you to love me more; if you don't ask me to love you less. (*Silence.*) Okay? (*Silence.*) Okay? (*Silence.*) Obviously, not okay. (*Silence.*) I don't believe this. (*Silence.*) You want me to leave? Is that what you're saying? (*Silence.*) You want me to pack up and leave? (*Silence.*) Ellis, don't do this. (*Touches her.*)

ELLIS. Don't touch me!

LYNNE. What!

ELLIS. Don't touch me! You always wanna talk things out! Talk things to death! I don't know how the hell we've lasted.

LYNNE. Because you chose me! I'm your friendly neighborhood dentist. That's why you chose me! You want me to reach down and wrench out your feelings because you don't have the guts to do it yourself. That's why you chose me! So don't give me "you over-analyze, you always want to confront, you always want to talk." Because you chose me! You want me out, I'm out!

ELLIS. When does the fucking pain stop!

LYNNE. When we're dead! (*LYNNE crosses out of scene to apron; furious. Paces angrily—1,2,3; 1,2,3; 1,2,3. Stops. Thinks. Marches back into room just as defiant.*) I don't care what you say, I'm not leaving!

ELLIS. Thank God.

LYNNE. (*Plops on floor, rests against bed. Neither looking at the other, exhausted.*) Wanna go to the desert?

ELLIS. They'll split us up, you know. For two weeks, they'll split us up.

LYNNE. Wanna sleep on it?

ELLIS. Why are you letting a four-year-old run your life? (*Without rancor, explaining.*) I hate your energy, you know. I don't want to, but I do.

(*LYNNE realizes the irony. Pause.*)

ELLIS. If I lose your strength; I lose everything.

LYNNE. Is that what this is about? Because I cried in the hospital? Because I got nutsy with a cop?

ELLIS. Yes. (*Thinks.*) No. (*Thinks.*) I think it's about Mom and last Friday.

LYNNE. What about Mom and last Friday? (*Beat.*) You got this far.

(*ELLIS hands her journal.*)

LYNNE. (*Addresses audience.*) This is what she wrote:

ELLIS. Today she held me while I cried. I'm thirty-eight years old and she held me while I cried and because she loves me she said, "It'll be okay." But it's not okay, I'm dying. (*Quietly.*) She's my mother. She should have magical powers, she should be able to make it better. But she can't make it better and I feel betrayed by her, not it— and I want to protect myself from her, not it. (*Angrier.*) I want to punish her. I want to punish her because she's not magical. I want to punish her because she's not all giving. I want to punish her because she's not God. She is merely, my mother. (*Beat.*) I want to deny her. I want to deny her the most serious thing I can deny her. I want to deny her "me." (*Hears the enormity of what she's said.*) I want to deny her me.

LYNNE. She how easy that was.

ELLIS. You're out of the will.

(*SOUND: Crickets and George Winston. LIGHTS: BLACKOUT, except for stars stretched across the horizon. A FLASHLIGHT bumps on. LIGHT picks up ELLIS [SL] writing in her journal with the help of Duracell. Knapsack by her side.*)

ELLIS. I slept out last night—the first time I've ever slept out under the stars. Actually, I didn't sleep; I didn't want to miss anything. (*Stops writing.*) I watched the stars traverse the sky from East to West—I don't think I ever really knew that—that the stars rise in the East and set in the West. And this morning, the best of all. This morning, I wanted to get up. I wasn't even afraid of snakes.

(*CROSS-FADE on LYNNE [SR] in advanced state of hypothermia. Random swatting. Pulls blanket around shoulders; to audience:*)

LYNNE. I can't believe I'm doing this. Out here. On some lousy hill. In the middle of the desert. In the middle of the night. Fasting to death and freezing my chaconees off. Frankly, I don't know how Christ did it. (*Slaps arm; SOUND of very loud coyote.*) Oh, swell. Explain this to my mother. "Your daughter was eaten alive by a pack of wild coyotes in the Mojave desert while becoming one with the universe. (*Slaps elbow.*) God, I'm hungry. Two more hours to breakfast. Probably tofu on toast. (*Slaps neck; CROSS-FADE.*)

ELLIS. (*Writes.*) There's this poem by some guy named Wang Zoo. (*Looks up.*) If a man's in a skiff heading for shore and an empty boat bumps into his, what does he do? He keeps on heading for shore. But if there's a person in the other boat, what does he do? He rants, he raves, he bellows, he kicks, and stops heading for shore. His ranting and raving won't change anything. But he's seduced into thinking it can. (*Beat.*) I sat in that boat and ranted away a lifetime and never got any closer to shore. It's become very clear I can't change what's about to happen. I can't hold back death. And the weirdest thing? There's a peacefulness in that. There's not a damn thing I can do. The joke is that was true with everything else in my life. The seduction was to think I could.

LYNNE. (*FLASHLIGHT crosses the stage. LYNNE sings a la Mister Rogers.*) "It's a *be*-oo-tiful day in the neighborhood, a beautiful day in the neighborhood. Could you be mine?

(*Enters ELLIS' light.*)

LYNNE. "Would you be mine?"

(*SUN begins to rise slowly.*)

ELLIS. What are you doing here!
LYNNE. That's what I've been asking myself for twelve days. Want to make sand castles, Chickee?
ELLIS. What if we get caught?
LYNNE. What are they gonna do? Lash us with a soba noodle? Take away our "I-Ching?" [Ee-ching]
ELLIS. How you doin'? (*Shivers.*)
LYNNE. (*Sits down next to her and shares the blanket.*) I'm having a lot of trouble with "unconditional love." For starters, I hate the cook.
ELLIS. God, it's good to see you.
LYNNE. It's good to see you saying, "It's good to see you." (*Flicks FLASHLIGHT on Ellis' face.*) Geez, Ellis, if I didn't believe in this stuff before I do now. You look radiant.

(*FLASHLIGHT off.*)

ELLIS. Last night, I dreamt I was sitting on a fence, teetering between choosing life and choosing death. I wanted to choose life ... but I was afraid of making a commitment. (*Beat.*) We shouldn't be doing this. We're supposed to keep silence.

LYNNE. We're here to make changes, right? I'm working on defying authority. What are you working on?

ELLIS. Trying to stop my terror of negative thoughts. I'm up to ten a day. (*Beat.*) Why do you think we keep death out of life?

LYNNE. There's pain in death.

ELLIS. There's pain in birth. What'll I do if the fear comes back?

LYNNE. Let it.

ELLIS. Let it?

LYNNE. Let it.

ELLIS. Gotcha. I need to itch.

LYNNE. Where?

ELLIS. My right shoulder.

LYNNE. (*Scratches Ellis' right shoulder.*) Boy, for someone who feared dependency.

ELLIS. Funny, isn't it? We'd never be together, you know. If I weren't dying (*Beat.*) And this whole year. This whole year. I've never been more alive. (*Beat.*) Why did you stay?

LYNNE. It never occurred to me to leave. (*Thinks.*) Because I love you. (*Beat.*) Because I fear dying alone.

ELLIS. You won't die alone.

LYNNE. Will you be there?

ELLIS. I'll be there. You won't die alone. My world; I make the rules.

LYNNE. (*Dives into Ellis' knapsack.*) Got any peanut butter in here?
ELLIS. You can cry.
LYNNE. It's selfish.
ELLIS. You can cry.

(*LIGHTS fade on BOTH as ELLIS exits with blanket.*)

LYNNE. (*Addresses audience.*) Now, I'm not dumb enough to suggest two weeks on a low mount in the high desert turned her life around. But when we got back everything had changed. Ellis made more phone calls, wrote more proposals, AD'd a live stage production for PBS, but when we walked in the woods, she dawdled. She seemed to have lost all fear. Fear of death, fear of life, fear of me. She even bought a pair of Mary Janes. A kind of symbolic break. Seemed delightfully ironic that Mary Janes became synonymous with "fuck you."

(*MUSIC starts softly, "Eye of the Tiger" from* Rocky III.*)

LYNNE. Benberg had said three months. It was now eighteen and rising. The cough was still there, her mouth was still dry, but the lump in the shoulder? It was going down. And waiting? Oh, had she learned to wait.

(*SOUND of music level rises to blasting. ELLIS enters and sits as LIGHTS come up on bench area now the*

---

* Mention is made of songs which are *not* in the public domain. Producers of this play are hereby CAUTIONED that permission to produce this play does not include rights to use these songs in production. Producers should contact the copyright owners directly for rights.

(*SOUND of music level rises to blasting. ELLIS enters and sits as LIGHTS come up on bench area now the waiting area in Houston. ELLIS has headphones on. Totally relaxed in chair, SHE colors and taps her foot to the music. LYNNE talks to her, no sound is heard. ELLIS is oblivious. LYNNE shrugs, sits; her movements unaffected by the music. NURSE EATON enters, walking counterpoint to the music; calls out a name, no sound is heard. ELLIS lifts headphones. SOUND out.*)

ELLIS. (*Yells to Lynne.*) What color looks good on Shirley Partridge!

(*NURSE EATON casts a glance. As SHE exits, LYNNE hastily scans waiting room; then reverts to her "mortified" slump. Surreptitiously whispers into Ellis' ear.*)

LYNNE. Housedress or when she's playing the tambourine?
ELLIS. (*Yells.*) Housedress!
LYNNE. (*In her ear.*) Try periwinkle blue. Want some soup?

(*ELLIS nods "yes," replaces headphones. SOUND on: "Tiger" again blares forth as SHE searches for periwinkle blue. LYNNE reaches for thermos behind bench, pours soup into top, nudges Ellis, ELLIS sets one speaker off ear, takes soup. SOUND out.*)

ELLIS. (*Yells.*) How long have we been waiting?
LYNNE. Four hours.
ELLIS. (*Yells.*) What's the record!
LYNNE. Mrs. Headley at nine.

ELLIS. (*Yells.*) Is this too loud?
LYNNE. (*Yells.*) No, but you are!

(*ELLIS anchors headphones around her neck; stares into her soup.*)

LYNNE. Oh God, you find a lump? Is there a lump? (*Looks into soup; sucks in breath in high outrage.*) One. One lump.
ELLIS. (*Laughs.*) Well, would I change in two years? (*Gets serious.*) You know, I was just thinking ... You were there when I had the hysterectomy, you were there when they diagnosed cancer, you were there when I overdosed. I was just thinking ...
LYNNE. What?
ELLIS. You're a fucking jinx.
LYNNE. Where'd you hear that one?
ELLIS. (*Coughing.*) Some guy in the chemo ward. (*Coughing gets worse.*) I can't get air. (*Beat.*) I can't get air.
NURSE EATON. (*Hurries in.*) What's wrong?
ELLIS. (*Gulps for air.*) Isn't that silly? (*Gulps air.*) I can't get air.

(*LIGHTS fade slightly. SOUND of muffled voices. MALE NURSE and NURSE rush in, clustering around Ellis, escort her into bed area. Another swirl of activity setting the next scene, i.e. MALE NURSE brings in blanketed cot; NURSE brings in IV pole; NURSE EATON attaches tubing to Ellis.*)

LYNNE. (*Crosses DS and addresses audience as frantic movements in the dark continue.*) Ellis began to vomit that night. And vomit and vomit. I was emptying basins as fast as I could run. Then the male nurse climbed on the bed and stuck a tube down her throat. She now had oxygen tubing in her nose, IV's in her arms, and tubing in her stomach. For someone who wanted freedom, she was attached like a Bill Baird marionette.

TRISH. (*Enters; hands Lynne gloves, mask and paper cup; helps her into isolation gown.*) Change whenever you enter her room. New mask, new gown, new gloves. Her white blood count's low.

LYNNE. They said a thousand.

TRISH. It's a hundred. Someone added an extra "0." (*Exits.*)

LYNNE. (*Dons gloves.*) I phoned her mother in Barnegat Bay but she was sick herself—her legs, arms rubbed raw from infection, a product of the sun. She died two months later of skin cancer, screaming for *her* mother. (*Beat.*) Three days later, I had a job interview, eighty miles out of town. I wanted to cancel but Ellis insisted; I didn't get back until late. On my return, I learned one thing very quickly. When someone becomes helpless, latent vultures begin to circle. And the healthy line up with the healthy.

(*LIGHTS full up. SOUND of gastric sump tube; SOUND of oxygen. ELLIS is lying in hospital bed on a forty-five degree angle to audience next to an US IV pole, bed table with chart, and chair. DS guardrail is up. There is a blanketed cot just below the window SC, paralleling the bed. ELLIS is connected to a bank of tubing: oxygen attached around the ears to her nose; IV's in her arm; sump tube in her nose. Her mouth is so dry from medicine, it's now affecting her speech. There are sheets on the floor, emesis basin and Kleenex on bed table. LYNNE enters wearing mask, carrying a paper cup.*)

LYNNE. Hi, Kiddo!
ELLIS. (*Relief.*) Oh, good.

LYNNE. Good what? Good to see me? (*Sits on bed.*)

(*ELLIS smiles "yes."*)

LYNNE. Oh, good. (*Offers her paper cup. Side-of-mouth, like a gangster.*) No one was looking, so I stole ya some ice chips.
ELLIS. Shh.
LYNNE. Shh, what? They're for your mouth.
ELLIS. Will it make them angry?
LYNNE. Make who angry?
ELLIS. Let'sh not make them angry, okay?
LYNNE. (*Puzzled; relents.*) Okay. (*Sets cup on table; leans over.*) Grab my neck.

(*ELLIS does. LYNNE pulls her up.*)

LYNNE. Scootch.

(*ELLIS does.*)

LYNNE. Better?
ELLIS. Yesh.
LYNNE. Here.

(*Hands ELLIS cup. ELLIS is hesitant. NURSE EATON enters from bathroom wearing isolation gown, no mask, gloves. Tucks in bedding.*)

NURSE EATON. She messed her bed again. Third time tonight. (*Loudly, as if chiding a small child.*) You've been a naughty girl, haven't you, Mrs. Crowley.
ELLIS. Yesh.
NURSE EATON. (*Loudly to Ellis; pointing to ice cup.*) Careful, or you'll spill your water. Did you spill

your water? (*Aside to Lynne.*) They don't make it easy, do they? (*Picks up emesis basis from bed table; exits to bathroom.*)

(*LYNNE stands dumbfounded.*)

NURSE EATON. (*Returns.*) Just when we'd finish cleaning her up. We'd clean her up again. (*Loudly to Ellis.*) You've really been a naughty girl. (*Walks to door. Intimately to Lynne.*) She just keeps shitting. (*Exits.*)

LYNNE. (*Continues to stare in disbelief at Nurse Eaton's receding back. Takes Kleenex from bed table, moistens it in ice cup, sits on bed, and dabs Ellis' mouth.*) You're bleeding again. Open wide. Can you open wide?

(*ELLIS does.*)

LYNNE. (*Dabs her mouth.*) She's treating you like you're two.
ELLIS. Poetic jushtish.
LYNNE. She's never done that before. She's never dared. (*Moistens Kleenex; dabs mouth.*) Your mouth's a mess. Am I hurting you? (*Beat.*) Should I steal some more peroxide? Can you gargle with peroxide? (*Beat.*) What are you thinking? (*Laughs.*) Well, would I change in two years?
ELLIS. We'll do thish again.
LYNNE. What again? "Us" again? (*Beat.*) In another life?

(*ELLIS nods "yes."*)

LYNNE. Think we'll know each other?
ELLIS. In a minute, Chickee. (*Silence; then like a tiny child.*) Let'sh go home.

LYNNE. Now?
ELLIS. Yesh, can we?
LYNNE. (*Sets ice cup on table.*) It's awfully late. Can we wait 'til tomorrow?

(*ELLIS thinks about it.*)

LYNNE. I promise. Tomorrow. If you still want to go. I'll spring you from this joint, okay? (*Beat.*) Your world. You makes the rules.

(*ELLIS blinks with both eyes.*)

LYNNE. Is that a wink? You telling me it's okay?

(*ELLIS nods.*)

LYNNE. Does it hurt to talk?

(*ELLIS nods.*)

LYNNE. In that case ... (*Looks at watch.*) It's 7:30. Time for "Family Feud."

(*With remote on bed table, LYNNE turns on television: "Family Feud" drones in the distance. ELLIS stares drowsily at TV. LYNNE sits on cot, focusing on Ellis. BOTH are very tired. LIGHTING change to suggest time change. SOUND: Fades out; fades in with theme from "Hill Street Blues."**)

---

* Mention is made of songs which are *not* in the public domain. Producers of this play are hereby CAUTIONED that permission to produce this play does not include rights to use

ELLIS. Oh, oh.
LYNNE. What?
ELLIS. I meshed the bed again.
LYNNE. (*Laughs.*) Oh, oh.
ELLIS. (*In little girl voice.*) Will she be mad?
LYNNE. She wouldn't dare.
ELLIS. Will she be mad?
LYNNE. It's not your fault.
ELLIS. I'll bet she'sh mad.
LYNNE. (*Beat.*) Tell you what. I'll clean you up, okay?
ELLIS. Better not.
LYNNE. She'll never know, I promise. She'll never know, okay? (*Beat.*) Would it embarrass you?
ELLIS. Not if you do it.
LYNNE. She'll never know, hang on. (*Rushes out.*)

(*SOUND of X-ray machine lumbering down the hall. SOUND of someone whistling [or semi-singing.] "Bye, Bye, Blackbird." A TECHNICIAN, wearing mask and gloves, rolls in [or mimes rolling in] a skeletal representation of a large* X-ray *machine, pushes it into position over the bed.*)

TECHNICIAN. (*Loudly.*) I have to take X-rays, Mrs. Crowley. (Plugs *it into* wall.) Can you sit up?

(*ELLIS maneuvers an inch.*)

TECHNICIAN. A little more?

---

these songs in production. Producers should contact the copyright owners directly for rights.

(*ELLIS tries.*)

TECHNICIAN. Here. (*Sets her in uncomfortable position: holding guardrail, staring out the side of the bed, like a Raggedy Ann doll.*) Okay, now hold that pose until I count ten. (*Leaves the room, whistling.*)

(*ELLIS falls out of position.*)

TECHNICIAN. (*Returns.*) Please, Mrs. Crowley, the sooner you hold, the sooner it's over.

(*ELLIS holds shakily onto rail. HE leaves the room. LYNNE hurries into doorway, carrying a ream of sheets.*)

TECHNICIAN. (*Offstage.*) You can't go in there! (*To Ellis.*) Now hold to ten. One, two, three, four ...

(*ELLIS holds, staring out the side of the bed. HE looks at watch; continues to whistle. ELLIS falls back.*)

TECHNICIAN. Did you hold to ten?
LYNNE. She held, you weren't counting.
TECHNICIAN. Maybe I'd better get another one.
LYNNE. She held, please, she held. (*Enters room, crosses into bathroom.*)

(*TECHNICIAN shrugs, unplugs machine, packs up, and exits whistling. LYNNE returns with washcloth and emesis basin filled with water.*)

LYNNE. Quick, roll on your side. Can you roll on your side?

(*ELLIS doesn't move.*)

LYNNE. (*Urgently.*) Roll on your side, chum.

(*ELLIS does with effort.*)

LYNNE. Here. (*Races around to DS side.*) Grab my arm. (*Nothing. Grabs Ellis' arm and pulls her on her side.*) Hold on to the guard rail, okay? (*Kneels down, puts Ellis' hands on guardrail.*)

(*ELLIS holds on like a child.*)

LYNNE. Okay, now roll over. Roll over a little more. (*Hurries around US side.*) A little more. Please, honey, a little more. (*Pulls out bottom sheet, balls it, tosses it on floor. Quickly cleans Ellis with washcloth.*) She won't be mad. She'll never know. Trust me. She'll never know.
ELLIS. Let'sh go home.
LYNNE. Tomorrow, okay? I promise, tomorrow. (*Picks up clean sheet; hears SOMEONE approaching.*) Roll back, someone's coming. Roll back, honey. (*Stashes clean sheet under cot blanket. While juggling the emesis basin, SHE grabs dirty sheets and races to bathroom.*)

(*ELLIS remains in the same position.*)

LYNNE. Roll back!

(*LYNNE exits. ELLIS falls back. MALE NURSE enters carrying a jug and a long needle; sets it on floor. LYNNE enters.*)

MALE NURSE. You'll have to leave now.
LYNNE. (*Almost laughs.*) What!

MALE NURSE. Doctor's going to do a lung tap. (*Studies chart.*) Sorry but you'll have to leave.

LYNNE. They let me stay before.

MALE NURSE. (*Disturbed by something on chart.*) Who let you stay?

LYNNE. Benberg.

MALE NURSE. For a lung tap?

LYNNE. For three lung taps.

MALE NURSE. (*Doesn't hear; preoccupied.*) When the doctor comes, you'll have to leave. (*Exits.*)

LYNNE. (*Moves quickly to bed.*) Hold on to the side. Hold on, okay? I need to put this sheet down.

(*ELLIS doesn't move.*)

LYNNE. If it's missing, they'll know. Hold on, okay? (*LYNNE hurries around to DS side of bed; pulls her toward guardrail.*) When the doctor comes, should I leave? Would it be easier for you if I left?

(*ELLIS shakes her head "no" over and over.*)

LYNNE. Okay, then hold on, okay? Just for a second. (*Runs around to US side.*)

(*ELLIS falls back.*)

LYNNE. Can't you hold on? (*Runs to DS side; pulls her toward guardrail.*) Please, Ellis, hold on. You have to help me. Hold on. (*Runs around to US side.*) Your eyes are so red. Are you overdosing again? Does it feel like an overdose?

(*ELLIS falls back.*)

LYNNE. Please, hold on! (*LYNNE shoulders Ellis up; forces sheet under.*) There! Good!

(*ELLIS falls back on bed in a slightly neck-breaking position: slumped down, below the pillow.*)

LYNNE. Grab my neck. (*Beat.*) Grab my neck. If she sees you, she'll know. Grab my neck. (*Leans down; puts Ellis' arms around her neck; tries to inch her toward the pillow.*) Now, scootch up. (*Beat.*) Just scootch like you always do. (*Tries to move her.*) You're dead weight. Can't you help me? Please, honey, hike up.

(*ELLIS tries hard, inches gained. LYNNE lets her head down slowly. It is now barely on the pillow. NURSE EATON enters with box of medicine. MALE NURSE follows with heparin needle; goes directly to Ellis, prepares catheter, administers heparin shot.*)

NURSE EATON. You'll have to leave now. (*Picks up jar and needle; sets it on bed table.*)
LYNNE. (*Rote.*) I won't get in his way.
NURSE EATON. I said, "You'll have to leave." (*Holds up box of medicine.*) For diarrhea. No side effects. It'll just make her mouth exceedingly dry.
LYNNE. You can't do that! Her mouth's so dry it's bleeding!
NURSE EATON. The fact remains, the doctor prescribed it.
LYNNE. Which doctor prescribed it?
NURSE EATON. (*Opens box of medicine.*) The doctor on duty.
LYNNE. He's never been in here!

NURSE EATON. The doctor prescribed it. She's getting dehydrated. Besides, we can't spend the night cleaning her up.

LYNNE. I'll clean her up. If it happens again, I'll clean her up.

NURSE EATON. (*Walks to tubing; unscrews bottle of medicine.*) That's not the point.

LYNNE. That is the point.

NURSE EATON. No, here's the point. The doctor prescribed it.

LYNNE. Then unprescribe it! Look at her mouth!

(*MALE NURSE takes needle out of catheter, inserts it again.*)

LYNNE. (*Attempts to calm down; addresses Male Nurse.*) They did that this morning. They did that at ten. (*Catches nervous look from MALE NURSE to Nurse Eaton.*) Didn't they do that at ten?

NURSE EATON. (*Fills eyedropper.*) You'll have to leave now.

LYNNE. (*Rote.*) They let me stay before.

NURSE EATON. (*Finality.*) I said, "You'll have to leave."

(*MALE NURSE takes needle, inserts it into catheter once again.*)

LYNNE. What's wrong? Is it clotted? (*Beat.*) Did they wait too long? Is it clotted?

(*MALE NURSE hurries to door; LYNNE follows.*)

MALE NURSE. If it's clotted, we'll unclot it. No cause for alarm. (*Exits.*)

LYNNE. I know, but is it clotted?

(*NURSE EATON opens sump tube to Ellis' stomach and is about to put medicine down it.*)

LYNNE. (*Rushes over, whips her hand over the tube, blocking it. SHE lowers her voice.*) I'm telling you, you're not giving her something that'll make her mouth dryer.

NURSE EATON. (*Same tone; medicine dropper poised.*) And I'm telling you, it's been prescribed.

LYNNE. What about her heparin, wasn't that prescribed? Wasn't that prescribed at ten?

NURSE EATON. You're getting emotional.

LYNNE. You bet I am. Wasn't that prescribed at ten!

NURSE EATON. (*Guides Lynne to apron.*) Okay, now calm down. Can we calm down?

(*LYNNE takes a deep breath.*)

NURSE EATON. Just calm down and listen, okay?

(*LYNNE does.*)

NURSE EATON. In my job I follow orders, I follow doctors' orders. I have no choice, I just obey. Understand? (*Waits.*)

(*LYNNE absently nods.*)

NURSE EATON. Good. Now. If a doctor prescribes medicine—whether or not I agree with that medicine—I have no choice, I just obey. Understand? (*Waits.*)

(*LYNNE nods.*)

NURSE EATON. Good. Now a doctor has ordered a lung tap. Not just any doctor, but a particular doctor, a particular doctor with a particular preference. So. (*Doesn't wait for Lynne to react.*) Before the doctor enters a room, he prefers I empty the room. Not your choice; not my choice; but his choice. Understand?

LYNNE. (*Quietly.*) Putting it that way, I can't help but understand. Of course, it's the doctor's choice. (*Beat.*) So. (*Beat.*) When the doctor enters the room, and finds my body still in the room, he can choose to leave the room; do a lung tap with me in the room; or , find a less particular doctor with a less particular preference who will let me stay in the room.

BLOOD NURSE. (*Barely enters room with caddy.*) I have to get a blood test, Mrs. Crowley.

LYNNE. (*Does not take her eyes off Eaton.*) Are you Christine!

BLOOD NURSE. No.

LYNNE. Get Christine!

(*BLOOD NURSE hurries out.*)

NURSE EATON. (*Explodes.*) You can't countermand a doctor's orders! You're not a relative! You have no say!

LYNNE. (*Hesitant; puzzled.*) I have power of attorney.

NURSE EATON. (*Pause.*) In that case ... (*Shrugs: "just doing my job."*) ... fine.

(*Puts eyedropper back in medicine bottle, screws on cap, without a trace of animosity. LYNNE watches—surprised by the power of her remark. NURSE EATON walks out, a study in composure.*)

LYNNE. You look so uncomfortable. Don't you care?

(*ELLIS stares into the distance, squinting, as if by focusing intensely with her outward eyes she can see her inner life.*)

LYNNE. Don't you care?

(*ELLIS makes an incomplete circle with her thumb and index finger, as if the index finger was stretching to touch the thumb.*)

LYNNE. What? (*Beat.*) A circle?

(*ELLIS shakes her head "no." Makes another incomplete circle with the index finger, stretching the index finger over and over, trying to touch the thumb.*)

LYNNE. A "C?"

(*SHE shakes her head "no." LYNNE finally begins to understand, brakes the urgency.*)

LYNNE. Your life? (*Beat.*) Is it closing?

(*SHE nods "yes."*)

LYNNE. Was it *all* sad?

(*ELLIS looks intently at Lynne; smiles shakes her head "no." Her breathing becomes irregular. Breathing in becomes weaker; breathing out becomes stronger and longer.*)

LYNNE. Ellis. (*Beat.*) Are you dying?

(*Long delays between each breath—as if there'll never be another.*)

LYNNE. I'm here, kiddo. I'm here.

(*Then there's another.*)

LYNNE. Go with it, chum. Let go.

(*Then nothing.*)

LYNNE. (*Takes off mask and gloves.*) I'm getting you out of here, chickee. We're going home. (*Peels the tape off Ellis' arm and removes the IV.*) We're blowing this joint, kiddo. (*Takes oxygen tubing out of her nose, the straps from around her ears.*) We're going home (*Walks out of scene; to audience.*) On a warm Monday morning in summer, driving south on the Jersey Turnpike, along the Jersey shore, I took Ellis home. To scatter her ashes at Island Beach, where we'd walked near the inlet at Barnegat Bay. (*Beat.*) I remembered our first drive to the shore— Ellis quoting from John's First Epistle: "There is no fear in love; but perfect love casteth out fear." I thought she was celebrating our friendship. (*Smiles.*) Little did I know she was trying to ward off sheer terror.

(*SOUND: of ocean and gulls.*)

LYNNE. I arrived at the entrance at 6 AM, but the barrier gate was down: "No cars allowed 'til eight." I'd have to hurry; I'd have to walk, to avoid the summer crowd. I figured it was six miles to the inlet, six miles back; a four-hour hike. I learned it was eleven miles to the inlet, eleven miles back; an eight-hour hike. (*Beat.*) I noticed everything on that walk: the blackbirds, the spikemoss. I was aware of a fly buzz, a friendly fly that followed me along the tarmac, darting in and out of the bramble. Seven-thirty jogged by, eight. I shifted my knapsack to my other shoulder—surprised by the weight. Why the inlet: why not any beach? No, Ellis wanted the inlet. I lost track of the fly. (*Beat.*) Eight-thirty, nine. A car went by; another car. Turn off, take any bay. Or you'll have ashes catching the wind in a maze of Frisbees. No, Ellis wanted the inlet. Another car, walk faster. Another car, let go. Nine-thirty, ten. The ashes slammed against my back. Another car, walk faster. Another car, let go. (*Beat.*) I turned off on a narrow pathway, climbed one sandy rise after another, until I gazed out at the morning ocean. The beach was deserted, the sea calm, the sky a Maxfield Parrish blue. And I knew Ellis wasn't minding this spot at all. (*Sits.*) I sat down on a ridge of sand ... (*Takes off shoes and socks.*) Took the box of ashes out of the tote bag, and shuddered. A friend said I'd see bone. (*Slowly pushes it open, like a cigar box.*) Inside was a clear plastic bag with a wire tie; inside that, the solidness of gray and white, salt and pepper. The fear left. (*Beat.*) I waded into the ocean, the water cold against my legs, undid the tie. I poured the ashes slowly between the waves. They swirled in the foam. Then I heard a voice from the deepest part of me, a voice that sounded very much like Ellis and it said, "Now, live." (*Beat.*) "Don't wait for Monday."

(*FADEOUT.*)

The End

Property Plot

Preset:
headphones (no cord)
phone on bed table
blanket and pillow on bed
one shirt, one man's shoe (extra large), one sock with hole in heel, on floor
coin changer under pillow
scrapbook under bed
grocery bag US of bed
bucket and brush (behind bench)

ACT I
bedspread and sheet (Ellis and male arm)
donut box (Ellis)
bathroom scale (Lynne)
journal (Ellis)
two lap blankets (Lynne)
two sketch pads (Lynne)
knapsack (Lynne)
two martini glasses (handsome German and another German)
two "1980" New Year's hats (handsome German and another German)
knapsack (Ellis)
Barnegat Bay quilt with reversible pattern (Ellis)
Kleenex tissues (Ellis)
knapsack containing baggie of trail mix and an address book (Ellis)
cigarette (Lynne)
white sheet (nurse)
suitcase (Helen)
manilla folder, pen, and journal (Ellis)
wheelchair (nurse)

clipboard (Nurse Eaton)
chair (nurse)
cowboy hat with peacock feather (Benberg)
file (Benberg)
blank paper (Benberg)
medical report (Trish)
clipboard (Trish)
subclavian kits: clear plastic bucket, t-tube, alcohol prep pad, tubex, heparin needle, op-site bandages (Farmer, Farmer's wife, Nurse Eaton, Ellis, Lynne)
pamphlets (Farmer, Farmer's wife, Lynne)
lectern or tray (Nurse Eaton)
catheter and heparin needle (Nurse Eaton)
hemostat (Nurse Eaton)
bath sheet-size bath towel (Ellis)
chair containing dressing kit (see description Act I), chux, prep pads, op-site bandage, hemostat, 2 packages of sterile rubber gloves, instructions (Lynne)
heparin tube, gauze, op-site (worn by Ellis)
mirror (Lynne)

ACT II

TV remote control and book on bed table
L.A. quilt
knapsack US of bed
thermos behind bench

box with Christmas wrapping (Helen)
bucket and Isocal pamphlet (Lynne)
the [vacuuming part of a vacuum cleaner] front part or hose from a vacuum cleaner (Ellis)
tray containing mug, heparin needle inserted into tubex, alcohol prep, and assorted socks (Helen)
heparin tube (worn by Ellis)

STARTING MONDAY 113

chart (Benberg)
clipboard and paper (Trish)
IV pole (attendant)
cot, blanket, and Ellis' robe (male nurse)
hospital bedclothes (nurse)
grocery bag containing toothpaste (giant-size tube), Haagan Daz ice cream carton, spoon (Lynne)
blood caddy (Blood Nurse)
journal (Ellis)
paper cup (Nurse Eaton)
parking ticket book and pen (L.A.Cop)
wheelchair (Lynne)
three or four pieces of clothing
paper and pencil (Helen)
paper cup (Lynne)
soup bowl (Lynne)
blanket (Lynne)
broom (Helen)
two flashlights (Lynne and Ellis)
knapsack (from US of bed) (Ellis)
coloring book (Ellis)
gloves, mask paper cup, isolation gown (Trish)
oxygen tubing (Ellis)
sheets on the floor
isolation gown, mask, gloves (worn by Nurse Eaton)
blanketed cot (male nurse)
IV pole (attendant)
emesis basin (nurse)
representation of X-ray machine (technician)
sheets (Lynne)
washcloth and emesis basin (Lynne)
jug with long needle for lung tap (male nurse)
eyedropper and medicine (Nurse Eaton)
prep pad, tubex and heparin needle (male nurse)

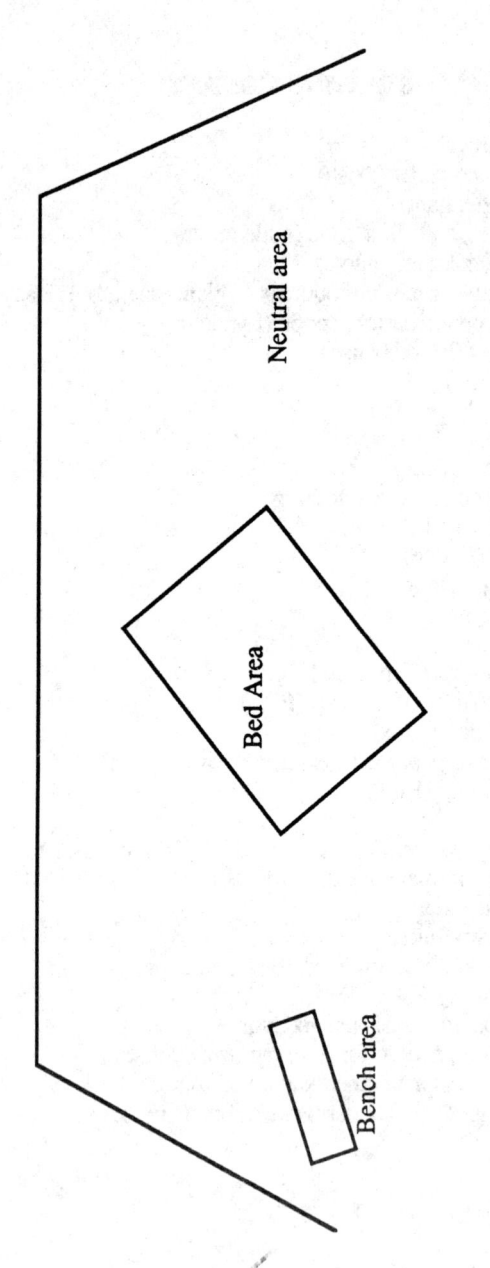

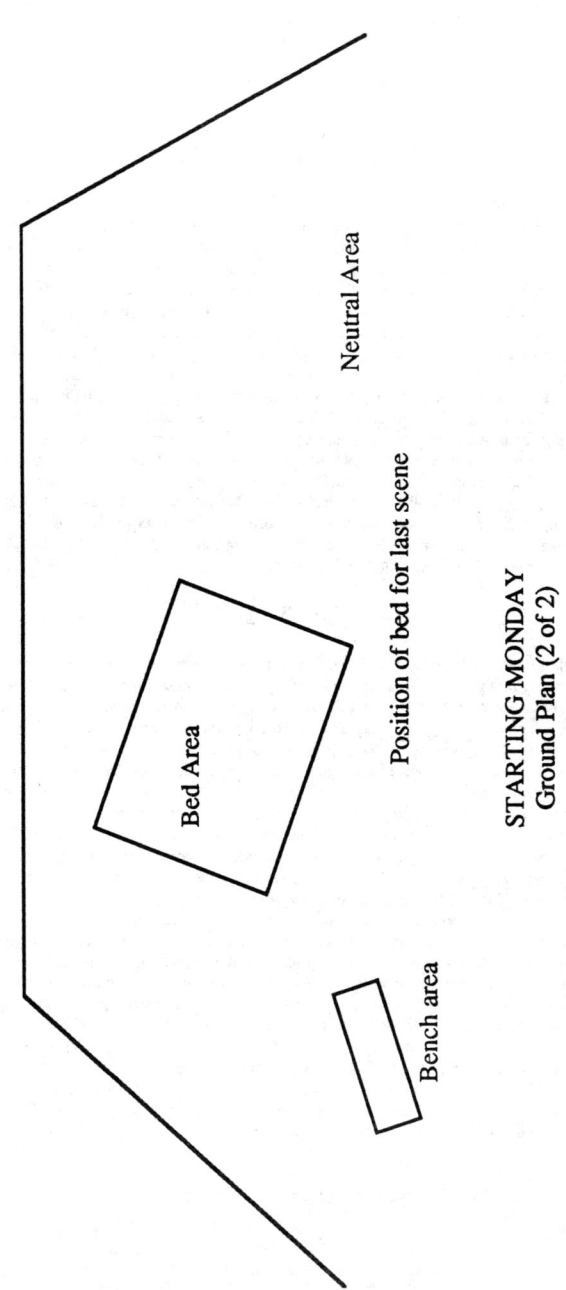

THE NORMAL HEART

(Advanced Groups.) Drama. Larry Kramer. 8m., 1f. Unit set. The New York Shakespeare Festival had quite a success with this searing drama about public and private indifference to the Acquired Immune Deficiency Syndrome plague, commonly called AIDS, and about one man's lonely fight to wake the world up to the crisis. The play has subsequently been produced to great acclaim in London and Los Angeles. Brad Davis originated the role of Ned Weeks, a gay activist enraged at the foot-dragging of both elected public officials and the gay community itself regarding AIDS. Ned not only is trying to save the world from itself, he also must confront the personal toll of AIDS when his lover contracts the disease and ultimately dies. This is more than just a gay play about a gay issue. This is a public health issue which affects all of us. He further uses this theatrical platform to plead with gay brethren to stop thinking of themselves only in terms of their sexuality, and that rampant sexual promiscuity will not only almost guarantee that they will contract AIDS; it is also bad for them as human beings. "An angry, unremitting and gripping piece of political theatre."—N.Y. Daily News. "Like the best social playwright, Kramer produces a cross-fire of life and death energies that illuminate the many issues and create a fierce and moving human drama."—Newsweek. $4.50. (Royalty $60-$40.) Slightly Restricted. (#788)

A QUIET END

(Adult Groups.) Drama. Robin Swados. 5m. Int. Three men—a schoolteacher, an aspiring jazz pianist and an unemployed actor—have been placed in a run-down Manhattan apartment. All have lost their jobs, all have been shunned by their families, and all have AIDS. They have little in common, it seems, apart from their slowing evolving, albeit uneasy, friendships with each other, and their own mortality. The interaction of the men with a psychiatrist (heard but not seen throughout the course of the play) and the entrance into this arena of the ex-lover of one of the three—seemingly healthy, yet unsure of his future—opens up the play's true concerns: the meaning of friendship, loyalty and love. By celebrating the lives of four men who, in the face of death, become more fearlessly life-embracing instead of choosing the easier path to a quiet end, the play explores the human side of the AIDS crisis, examining how we choose to lead our lives—and how we choose to end them. "The play, as quiet in its message as in its ending, gets the measure of pain and love in a bitter-chill climate."—N.Y. Post. "In a situation that will be recognizable to most gay people, it is the chosen family rather than the biological family, that has become important to these men. Robin Swados has made an impressive debut with *A Quiet End* by accurately representing the touching relationships in such a group."—N.Y. Native. (Royalty $60-$40.) Music Note: Samuel French, Inc. can supply a cassette tape of music from the original New York production, composed by Robin Swados, upon receipt of a refundable deposit of $25.00, (tape must be returned within one week from the close of your production) and a rental fee of $15.00 per performance. Use of this music in productions is optional. (#19017)

OTHER PUBLICATIONS FOR YOUR INTEREST

COASTAL DISTURBANCES
(Little Theatre- Comedy)

by TINA HOWE

3 male, 4 female

This new Broadway hit from the author of *PAINTING CHURCHES, MUSEUM,* and *THE ART OF DINING* is quite daring and experimental, in that it is *not* cynical or alienated about love and romance. This is an ensemble play about four generations of vacationers on a Massachusetts beach which focuses on a budding romance between a hunk of a lifeguard and a kooky young photographer. Structured as a series of vignettes taking place over the course of the summer, the play looks at love from all sides now. "A modern play about love that is, for once, actually about love--as opposed to sexual, social or marital politics . . . it generously illuminates the intimate landscape between men and women." --NY Times. "Enchanting."--New Yorker. #5755

APPROACHING ZANZIBAR
(Advanced Groups—Comedy)

by TINA HOWE

2 male, 4 female, 3 children --Various Ints. and Exts.

This new play by the author of *Painting Churches, Coastal Disturbances, Museum,* and *The Art of Dining* is about the cross-country journey of the Blossom family--Wallace and Charlotte and their two kids Turner and Pony--out west to visit Charlotte's aunt Olivia Childs in Taos, New Mexico. Aunt Olivia, a renowned environmental artist who creates enormous "sculptures" of hundreds of kites, is dying of cancer, and Charlotte wants to see her one last time. The family camps out along the way, having various adventures and meeting other relatives and strangers, until, eventually, they arrive in Taos, where Olivia is fading in and out of reality--or is she? Little Pony Blossom persuades the old lady to stand up and jump up and down on the bed, and we are left with final entrancing image of Aunt Olivia and Pony bouncing on the bed like a trampoline. Has a miracle occurred? "What pervades the shadow is Miss Howe's originality and purity of her dramatic imagination."--The New Yorker. #3140

Other Publications for Your Interest

CAT'S PAW
(LITTLE THEATRE—DRAMA)
By WILLIAM MASTROSIMONE

2 men, 2 women—Interior

This is a gripping drama about terrorism; but it does not come at the subject in a way you'd expect. When we think of "the terrorist", we generally think of a wild-eyed religious or political fanatic. What if, posits the acclaimed author of *The Woolgatherer, Extremities, Shivaree* and *Nanawatai*, a terrorist came along who was brilliant, who was articulate and who was *right*? Victor is the head of a terrorist group which is responsible for a bomb attack against the White House in which 27 people have been killed. He has arranged to have a television news reporter led to his lair, there to tell the world why he has done what he has done. Victor's obsession is the destruction of the world's water supply, and with it the final destruction of the human race, by pollution. When the reporter asks him if he feels any guilt about the death of the 27 innocent people, he replies that hundreds of innocent people are dying every hour because of what mankind is doing to its water supply—and do the people responsible feel guilt for this? This cat-and-mouse game between the young woman reporter and Victor gets more and more tense, leading to a shocking and violent conclusion. A standing-room-only hit at Seattle Repertory Theatre and later at San Diego's Old Globe. "An agonizingly suspenseful thriller."—San Diego Tribune. "A grabber."—Seattle Times. "Timely, thought-provoking and definitely worth seeing."—San Diego Reader. "Entertaining, informative, thoughtful and scary."—The Weekly (Seattle). (#5056)

SHIVAREE
(LITTLE THEATRE—COMIC DRAMA)
By WILLIAM MASTROSIMONE

2 men, 3 women—Combination interior

We are delighted to publish this lesser-known but wonderful play by the acclaimed author of *Extremities* and *The Woolgatherer*. The story concerns a young hemophiliac youth named Chandler who has been kept, of necessity, by his cab driver mother in a very sheltered sort of existence. Chandler is desperate for contact with the world. He is also highly intelligent; but is supremely naive about the ways of the world. He pays a neighbor to bring him a girl; but he can't go through with his plans to have sex with her. He just doesn't know what to do about his craving for love—until he meets Shivaree. She is another neighbor who supports herself by being an itinerant belly-dancer. She is a True Original, and before too long the delightful Shivaree and the innocent Chandler are in love, much to the consternation of Chandler's mother, who forbids Chandler to ever see Shivaree again, throwing Shivaree out of Chandler's room. Chandler, undaunted, climbs out the fire escape—his first venture outside his hermetic world—going after his love. Fans of Mr. Mastrosimone's other plays will recognize the true-ness of the characterizations and the poignancy and humor of typical Mastrosimone dialogue in this wonderful play. (#21689)

Other Publications for Your Interest

DOMINO
(ADVANCED GROUPS—COMIC DRAMA)
By ROBERT LITZ

6 men, 1 woman to play various roles/Unit Set.

This "excruciatingly funny political comedy" (N.Y. Post) is about a rather thick U.S. foreign loan banker who visits a Central American banana republic, supervised by a charmingly cynical C.I.A. operative, to renegotiate a 3.8 billion dollar debt. Unwittingly, he winds up financing and masterminding the overthrow of the government. Written in short, hilarious scenes (well, "hilarious" in a rather frightening way...) *Domino* has a lot to tell us about what what is really going on in these days of Contras, Sandinistas and Noriegas. "Hostages are taken; prisoners are tortured; ransoms are paid; weapons are hijacked; drugs are traded; political deals are struck—and press conferences are held to celebrate the whole sordid mess. Then, when the C.I.A. discovers a more expedient way to sell off the country to capitalist interests, everybody betrays everybody else, and the whole cycle is played all over again. After a while you can't tell the corrupt generals from the bought-out guerillas. And if there ever was a hero, or an honest idealist, in the house, somebody shot him."—N.Y. Post. $4.00

(#6165)

EL SALVADOR
(LITTLE THEATRE—DRAMA)
By RAFAEL LIMA

6 men, 1 woman—Interior.

This brilliant new naturalistic drama from NYC's famed Circle Repertory takes place in a hotel room in El Salvador which has been converted into a home base for a dissolute and mostly disillusioned gaggle of U.S. TV journalists, fed up with the futility of constantly risking their lives reporting on a revolution that nobody back home cares about. Not that *they* care much, either—but it does give them something to talk about. The play takes place on a day when the El Salvador military, flying sophisticated helicopters provided them by the U.S. government, have bombed a small remote village, killing many civilians, including women and children. That night, as they wait out an attack on the capital and, possibly, on the hotel, the crew members talk of their feelings about the war, their shame about America's role in it, and their separation from loved ones far away. "A tensely fascinating evening in the theatre."—N.Y. Post. "*The Front Page* transposed to a Third World war zone."—Village Voice. "A powerful, gripping drama...has the ring of authenticity that is as vivid as reality. You are absolutely there."—UPI. "Lima knows his subject and has illuminated it with pungent dialogue and crackling theatricalism."—N.Y. Daily News.

(#7024)

Other Publications for Your Interest

THE VOICE OF THE PRAIRIE
(LITTLE THEATRE—COMIC/DRAMA)
By JOHN OLIVE

2 men, 1 women—to play a variety of roles
May be done with up to 10 actors—Unit Setting

When this play begins, we are listening to an old hobo (named "Poppy" by his avid companion young Davey Quinn) tell a tall tale. It is the early 1890's, and itinerant story tellers such as Poppy really were the voices of the prairie. Many years later, when Davey is grown up, he is "discovered" by radio entrepreneur Leon Schwab, telling his tales of Poppy and of Frankie the Blind Girl, whom he rescued from a cruel father and with whom he went on a cross-country adventure. Schwab thinks Quinn's stories would attract an audience for radio, the "wave of the future". Sure enough, David Quinn becomes famous as the Voice of the Prairie, as the cleverly-constructed play cross-cuts between scenes of Leon and David and scenes of young Davey and Frankie the Blind Girl, on the lam, in search of adventure. These scenes culminate in the unfortunate separation of Davey and Frankie, as Frankie is recognized, captured and sent back home. David Quinn, the grown-up Voice of the Prairie, has not seen or heard from her since; until, that is, Leon locates her in hopes of using his discovery of the actual, famous Frankie the Blind Girl for its sentimental value, to keep the new F.C.C. off his back. Will David forgive Frankie for leaving him so many years ago? Will Frankie agree to help Leon avoid jail for broadcasting without a license? "Endearing."—N.Y. Times. "That rare thing: a small, skillful play with a deft heart."—Los Angeles Times. "Beguiling entertainment and as American as corn."—Hartford Advocate. "First-rate entertainment. I can't remember when I last so enjoyed a play."—Torrington Register Citizen. Slightly Restricted.

(#24047)

CARELESS LOVE
(LITTLE THEATRE—DRAMA)
By JOHN OLIVE

1 male, 1 woman—Unit set

What a terrific little play for an actress and actor to sink their teeth into! And, it's about something that matters: committment, and responsibility, in love. When we first meet Jack, he is an aspiring actor, serious about his career but not very serious about his girlfriend, Martha, a waitress who is an aspiring dancer, who is a lot more serious about Jack. The couple drifts along on a cloud of good times — until Martha gets pregnant, at which time a *Choice* must be made. As the debate over their options progresses, Jack's acting career starts to take off; and, he starts to think more seriously about his life and his responsibilities. Unfortunately, at the same time Martha has been driven into self-absorption by Jack's carelessness, and has made a decision which is right for her, she thinks: she has decided to give the child up for adoption. So — at just about the time Jack is ready to make an emotional committment to Martha and to their child, it is too late: Martha has had the baby and put it up for adoption. This was, after all, *her* decision to make. Right? In the end, Martha is a self-sufficient contemporary woman, who makes her own choices. It is Jack who will hurt forever, from the pain of eternal separation from his child. "Bittersweet." — Variety. "In the delicacy of its writing, in the truth of its details...it is a most lovely, most satisfying evening in the theatre."—Chicago Tribune. "A lovely little play...works a winsome magic."—Philadelphia Daily News.

(#5237)